international
LANDSCAPE
DESIGN

Architecture of Gardens, Parks, Playgrounds & Open Spaces

Margaret Cottom-Winslow

Library of Applied Design

An Imprint of

PBC INTERNATIONAL, INC. ✦ NEW YORK

Distributor to the book trade in the United States and Canada:

Rizzoli International Publications Inc.
300 Park Avenue South
New York, NY 10010

Distributor to the art trade in the United States and Canada:

PBC International, Inc.
One School Street
Glen Cove, NY 11542
1-800-527-2826
Fax 516-676-2738

Distributed throughout the rest of the world:

Hearst Books International
1350 Avenue of the Americas
New York, NY 10019

Library of Congress Cataloging-in-Publication Data

Cottom-Winslow, Margaret
    International landscape design: architecture of gardens,
    parks, playgrounds, and open spaces / Margaret Cottom-
    Winslow.
            p.   cm.
    Includes index.
    1. Landscape architecture. 2. Landscape architecture --
    Pictorial works. I. Title.
    SB472.C68 1991   90-28473
    712 -- dc20   CIP
    ISBN 0-86636-137-5

CAVEAT—Information in this text is believed accurate, and will
pose no problem for the student or the casual reader.
However, the author was often constrained by information
contained in signed release forms, information that could
have been in error or not included at all. Any misinformation
(or lack of information) is the result of failure in these
attestations. The author has done whatever is possible to
insure accuracy.

For information about our audio products, write us at:
Newbridge Book Clubs, 3000 Cindel Drive, Delran, NJ 08370

Color separation, printing and binding by
Toppan Printing Co. (H.K.) Ltd. Hong Kong

Typography by
Graphique, Ltd.

10 9 8 7 6 5 4 3 2 1

ACKNOWLEDGMENTS

Each book has a unique genesis. In the case of this particular volume, the genesis began with my editor, Kevin Clark, who felt a volume on gardens and landscape design would be a companion piece and counterfoil to our latest effort concerning the effects of architecture on the environment. It was and is a splendid idea. With Kevin's patience, direction and acquiescence, this germ of an idea evolved beyond gardens per se, to encompass the whole — we hope! — of landscape architecture. That effort in and of itself has proved an informative, formidable and truly exciting task.

One of the more exciting aspects was that in my study of various projects and my research into the field, I often found it difficult to distinguish between what is architecture and what is landscape architecture. In the final analysis, I'm not sure where the dividing line exists — or even if there is one. I'd like the reader to consider whether our definitions might be artificial.

Those people who listened to this thesis of where these boundaries might lie were of inestimable help in finding my way through some of the quagmires and bogs of which projects to include and which to save for yet another volume and another topic. The wealth of material I received has made some of the choices difficult. And in this there are some individuals to whom I owe a debt: Howard Juster, who gave his time and suggestions, critiques and insightful comments; M. Paul Friedberg, who contributed his time, work and support; Theodore Osmundson, who wrote the gracious forward; and Lore Steinborn of the International Federation of Landscape Architects who put me in touch with many of those whose talents are illustrated in this book. Bedelia Hill has been able to deal with their idiosyncrasies — and mine — with humor and efficiency. I hope I have done them justice. Lastly, my agent Richard Barber must be acknowledged. His unfailing ability to listen to, and help me refine my ideas and directions is invaluable.

My first editor, Paul Brandwein, taught me that no author writes a book alone. Ideas must be articulated and refined, developed or abandoned, focused or be left for the reader to ponder. In my efforts I'm fortunate to have an editor who directs and appreciates, and an agent who is supportive and resourceful. Also, in terms of subject matter and contributions, this book has been a joy!

CONTENTS

FOREWORD

The International Federation of Landscape Architects is delighted that this book is being published and in so grand a fashion. For a profession to be effective it must be understood and recognized for its full worth. Although landscape architecture as an independent profession has had an important history for many years, its full scope and accomplishments have been little known, even by knowledgeable design professionals, but even less so by the general public. Perhaps this has been because the profession is so broad in scope, ranging from garden design to the regional landscape, that only those projects most easily recognized and noticed — gardens — have been thought for many years to be the sole province of landscape architects.

From the decade of the 1950s, this profession has moved steadily forward, applying its great talents to more and more of the world's man-made development and gradually but steadily adding its special sensitivity, understanding and technical training of land use and design to the broader landscape. More recent worldwide alarm concerning air and water pollution, destruction of wildlife habitat, and desertification of vast areas of formerly arable or forested lands have forced governments to seek, often in desperation, trained expertise to deal with complex and often interlocking environmental problems. Landscape architecture is one of those areas of expertise and it is being fast recognized as such.

The work of landscape architects in the domain of the garden abounds in print. The work of this profession, whose activities over the past three decades have burgeoned in the design and renovation of public and private areas of the urban and suburban environment, is only now being recognized and published in the more permanent medium of books. This publication is one of the first of these. And what a wonderfully rich document it is! As such, in full color, it is a strikingly successful testament to what the urban environment can be, when talented and highly competent landscape architects are given the task of creating outdoor areas for people.

Responding to new demands, landscape designers have developed techniques of public participation in developing user sensitive programs for projects of all kinds and designing to meet these demands. But within the context of practical urban use, the art of landscape design has asserted itself as well in striking and exciting places as well as relaxing and meditative expressions in creativity. This book runs the whole range, from the grand park to intimate urban gardens tucked behind buildings or clinging to rooftops of tall buildings.

It is a visually exciting book as well as one which probes why and how these works of the landscape art came into being. It is a major exposition of the human and ecological richness of what can happen when people in a society choose to make their surroundings not only useful but spiritually enriching.

We welcome the opportunity this book affords everyone to see, all in one place, what they can seldom witness in so many diverse locations around the world. It proves also that the landscape art knows no geographical boundaries. It satisfies the longing within people everywhere for a more beautiful and orderly world.

Theodore Osmundson, FASLA
President, International Federation of Landscape Architects

Redefining an Art

The Influence of our Beginnings

The natural landscape, not the man-made urban scape, is what defines the beginning of our planet as we know it. In many mythologies of creation, one God or many Gods create a world of plants and seas and rivers and mountains and deserts — and eventually of human beings. According to many religions, myths and legends, the life of mankind began in a garden — at least in an area of open, natural vegetation. The Old Testament, followed by Christians, Jews and Moslems, states that man started life in the Garden of Eden. Buddhism has Buddha meditating in a garden under a pipal tree with his hand on the earth so that it may bear witness to his enlightenment. And, it's said that when Buddha died the trees shed their leaves. Many so-called primitive cultures also believe that certain forms of vegetation can interact with the Gods. In fact, they believe that certain trees and plants are gods or forms of gods, and can perform magic — or at the very least, heal with leaves or bark or roots.

From this it would seem that the concept of "growing," of renewal, of cycles and seasons is common to many cultures and their mythologies. Perhaps because this concept reminds us of our own seasons and cycles and mortality. Even if we inhabit the most mechanized and urbanized of environments, we never quite lose sight of our rural and primeval beginnings, be it in the house plants we nourish or the natural forms we use as the inspiration for our industrialized forms.

We might also consider that the natural landscape is a physiological necessity. The oxygen produced by plants through photosynthesis is necessary for our survival. That designers have begun to realize this is evident in the time and attention spent incorporating the natural landscape into the man-made design fabric.

IN THE BEGINNING

It's also important to recognize that the "garden," the pastoral landscape, was our first home and perhaps still remains our first psychological and sub-conscious loyalty. If this is true, perhaps Landscape Design — Landscape Architecture — is a far older profession than even Architecture. Think about it. Which did man create first? Shelter or gardens? It might be argued that man first inhabited existing shelters and created gardens. He used caves for shelter and then planted gardens and cultivated a few crops outside the caves. Perhaps his first "structures" were for ritualistic purposes — not for shelter.

Let's consider for a moment those great ritualistic wonders of the ancient world, the megaliths, concerning which the *Larousse Encyclopedia of Prehistoric & Ancient Art* states:

> With megaliths, prehistoric man learned the art of architecture: not only do the horizontal stones of the dolmens foreshadow the lintel, but an overall plan is visible in the alignments of menhirs.

Perhaps the megaliths are a *form* of architecture in that they are an orderly arrangement and a design; but do these megaliths — Stonehenge, Castle Rigg, Carnac, Moel Ty Uchaf, Callanish — provide shelter or enclose space? As ritualistic and/or memorial designs, perhaps they fit more into the realm of landscape architecture. Because, in point of fact, the term "landscape architect" did not come into common usage until the late nineteenth and early twentieth centuries and the work of Frederick Law Olmsted. With these somewhat provocative ideas in mind, we might redefine some of our ancient monuments in the light of the present day and present conventions as to what constitutes architecture and what constitutes landscape architecture.

The point of this book and its focus, however, is not to upset preconceived categories, but rather to re-focus on what, indeed, is landscape design — landscape architecture. Many people and many different categories of professionals are involved in altering the natural landscape, in reforming, replanting, redefining and reusing the land as it exists today. For this reason, it might be well to reexamine our definitions.

Perhaps narrowly defining forms of landscape design as belonging to one discipline or the other creates divisions which are counterproductive to our preservation and use of what nature offers us. An understanding of the fine lines that separate architecture from landscape architecture might be in order. One might define landscape design as "all the design that takes place beyond the walls of the building." Even this definition, however, could be too restrictive. Into what category does the indoor atrium space fall?

THE CREATORS & THEIR CREATIONS
Individuals who have altered their own small plots of land for their own pleasure are not represented in this volume. All the work represented is by professionals — those who make their living designing and altering the natural environment: Landscape Architects, Architects, Playground Designers, Industrial Designers and others.

In terms of the choices of work, naturally that is somewhat subjective, but it is also representative of what constitutes the broad spectrum of Landscape Design. If you include as part of the landscape everything you see from where ever you are, whether you're standing still or in a moving vehicle, that's a very broad spectrum. But for ease of understanding and categorization the examples have been broken up into the following categories:

> Private Spaces
> Interactive Spaces
> Public Spaces
> Community Planning
> Inspirational & Historic Spaces

Within each of these categories, the examples are broken up into specific types, so that Private Spaces includes Individual Gardens, Estate Gardens, Roof Gardens & Playgrounds, Hotel & Resort Grounds and Gardens for Multiple Dwellings.

Interactive Spaces includes those areas designed to bring people together for sharing experiences, either with each other or with areas of the natural environment. These spaces include Vest-Pocket Parks, Atriums & Indoor Gardens, Corporate & Industrial Complexes, Civic, Cultural & Nature Centers and Campus Grounds & Masterplans.

Public Spaces are very much what they imply. Parks & Playgrounds, Sports & Games Complexes, Public Gardens, Plazas & Urban Squares and Exposition Parks & Zoos make up the majority of these examples.

Community Planning is perhaps more complex in that these examples are, for the most part, large-scale projects that sometimes are harder to illustrate with just a few drawings and photographs. Regional & Town Planning, Circulation Corridors (transportation & utility right-of-ways), Waterways, Land Reclamation Projects and Multi-Use Gardens will be included under this heading.

This last category, Inspirational & Historic Spaces, is perhaps the oldest category we include. A few of the examples are prehistoric, and the designers have been charged with the task of crowd control, parking and, in many cases, preservation of these monuments. Not always an easy task. Besides these National Parks & Geographic Wonders, Sculpture Gardens, Monuments & Memorials, Cemeteries and Meditative Spaces make up this chapter.

NATURAL MATERIALS & BUILDING BLOCKS
In landscape design, the designer arranges the land and objects upon it for man's enjoyment and use. But in many designs there is a significant difference between architectural design and landscape design. The most important difference is that plants grow. When an architect conceives of a building, it is, for the most part, a static construction. Yes, he or she knows that certain materials will weather, change color, erode and, over hundreds of years, decay. But, generally, the building is not expected to increase in size, flower, go to seed and regenerate. In most landscape designs that is precisely what is expected to happen. A landscape design is a living, growing, evolving organism.

Hence the first building material of the landscape designer — plant materials.

Besides plant materials you also have earth. You can alter earth, form it, berm it, excavate, pile, sculpt it. But only within the limits nature imposes. If the angles you choose are too steep, you have landslides. Earth has its own criteria, depending upon the composition of the soil. So, like plant materials, earth evolves and settles and allows the designer certain freedoms to alter it and form it. But always within the limits that the Earth decides.

What are the other elements that make up the palette of the landscape designer? Rock, water, concrete, stone, brick, wood, tile, metal, plastic, glass — many, many man-made materials are often used in conjunction with natural materials. They can often be stretched to limits unheard of in natural materials and forms, such as rocks and water.

Rocks, of course, can be broken and pulverized, and made smaller into pebbles, sand and the like. Rocks can be massed together and made larger. But how, indeed, do you control water and subjugate it to the demands of the designer? By designing its beds and channels, pools and waterfalls. By pumps, ponds, streams, lakes and dams. But man cannot truly alter the essence of water, anymore than he can alter the essence of plant materials, rock and the Earth.

In landscape design it's important to remember that the natural materials of the landscape designer may be, for the most part, immutable; but they are not inert, not static. They grow, move, evolve and erode. The landscape is always in flux.

CREATING SPACE — Using the Dynamic Ebb & Flow

The essence of the majority of landscape designs is, of course, altering and defining space. To do this, and to use the elements of plant materials, earth, rock, water and man-made materials, the designer has a number of components to play with and make use of in actualizing his or her vision, and that of the client — Space, Mass, Line & Direction, Color, Light & Shade, Texture, Scent, Time and Movement. In this palette of design components, perhaps Time and Movement are the most significant in landscape design.

The concept of Time incorporates the seasons, the revolutions of the earth around the sun, the juxtaposition of the planets, the climate, growth and change. All those variations in the cycles of nature that are immutable and yet constantly in change. Try to picture Stonehenge, for example, without the sun and stars in certain positions on certain days of the year. Imagine the garden without the sundial, or sunflowers that can't turn toward the sun. All the wonders of the earth are at the designer's fingertips when time is used as a component of the design palette. And, of course, there is that wondrous evolution of the seed

into the flower. That passage of time that produces the unfolding, brilliant, moist blossom from the dry, withered little seed.

Plant forms and plant masses can help create the Spatial Definitions the designer envisions. Along with rocks, water, earth forms and man-made materials for walls and fences, plants can form the real or imagined barriers that help to create the "floors," "walls," and sometimes even "ceilings" of the landscaped space.

Line, however, is a more difficult design component to identify in landscape design. Edges can perhaps serve as Line, and paving patterns can create Directional Elements. But true line as the two-dimensional representation of a three-dimensional object seldom exists in nature. Thrust and direction and ways to lead people down definitive paths, however, are a part of the design process. In this process of moving through the garden in the direction the designer provokes, we are again in the landscape of time. The viewer, the user, the inhabitant of the garden, the open space, moves through the space in Time.

This concept brings us to Movement as part of the design palette. This is one of the crucial differences between architectural design and landscape design. Plant materials move not only in their growth patterns and seasonal cycles but in the wind and even in gentle breezes. Water is constantly in motion by its very nature. Both water and plant materials are organic, living entities. The landscape, the garden, is also an organic, living entity that moves, grows, and is ever changing, not just in light and shadow but in actual form.

With growth and climate changes, Textures and Colors change. The landscape design must not only be sensitive to what the space looks like today, when the design is installed and finished — he or she must also take into consideration what this design will be in a year, in ten years, in twenty years — perhaps a hundred years from now.

CRUCIAL DECISIONS — The Perfect Placement

With all of these elements and design components the designer of the landscape has a wealth of tools to choose from. So how does this designer

make those perfect decisions that create balanced spaces and provide the serene gardens, the playing fields, the beautifully arborized boulevards, the populated urban plazas that we so desire to make our lives more useful and less stressful? Through creativity — and through the knowledge of the climate, the soil and other technical considerations that draw on scientific and technological knowledge.

Landscape design, like architectural design, is a synthesis of aesthetics and technology. The design is concerned with Rhythm & Balance, Unity & Variety, Accent & Contrast, Scale & Proportion. But other considerations play an equal part in the decisions the designer makes. How much shelter from the elements is necessary? What plant materials grow best in this particular climate? How will the design affect the ecosystem? How will adequate drainage be accomplished? How will erosion be prevented? And perhaps the most important consideration of all: how will the needs of the clients, the people using this space, be met?

Landscape design, the way man alters the earth is, after all, for human inhabitants who have certain needs, certain limitations. Landscape design is not sculpture. A design may incorporate sculpture, but to be truly useful and effective, it cannot be just a sculptural monument. Landscape design, after all, is for people to use and enjoy. It must incorporate life — living beings, humans and animals, as well as plant life.

OUR CULTURAL EXPRESSIONS — A Living Time Line

There are, however, other, less tangible considerations that the designer of the landscape, knowingly or unknowingly, takes into consideration — the society and culture in which he or she lives. All design is, in some measure, a reflection of society at a given point in time.

In the history of garden design, for example, it's interesting to compare the ancient gardens of the Near East — Egypt, Babylon, Assyria, Persia — and contemplate that almost all examples were either for the wealthy or incorporated into the sacred — temple gardens and the like. There were no gardens for the average man, no plazas, urban squares or playgrounds for the general populace.

The same was true in Greece and Rome, with the minor exception that some gardens have been found in small villas. Of course, to have even a small villa in those days probably took a certain amount of money, so we're still dealing with gardens only for those with some financial standing in the community.

In the Islamic world much the same was true. The wealthy and influential were fortunate enough to have gardens. Water, of course, was an extremely important element to combat the dry, often harsh arid climates of the Middle East, North Africa and Southern Europe. Even the colors favored by the Islamic designers — blues, turquoises, greens — reflected their need for, and appreciation of, water as an important element in the garden.

The Middle Ages brought the garden to Europe, but only in an exclusive, inward-looking capacity. The cloistered herb gardens of monasteries and convents were developed during this era. The average man may have benefited medicinally from the herbs grown in these cloisters, but only the common man lucky enough to venture inside these religious retreats could benefit from the serene sanctuary. On the other hand, plazas were being formed, perhaps without conscious intent, in front of cathedrals. Everyone could come to see the religious plays and listen to the strolling troubadours. It was a beginning.

The fourteenth century saw the development of the grand gardens of the Mughal Empire in India with meadows, water and flowers. These wonderful designs are often depicted in their "garden carpets." Farther east, in China and Japan, however, the garden had always been an important component of life. The symbolic aspects of the elements of garden design were important in religious practices, and each garden was laid out and tended with a care and reverence that was deeply entwined with both religious and cultural practices.

As these photographs show, each element was carefully chosen to accomplish a specific purpose. The designers of these gardens also chose specific elements to signify their intent. The two "Stone Gardens" — the "Daisen-in" and "Ryuan-ji" Temples — use a minimum of plant materials in the gravel and rock enclosures. Each seems to promote contemplation and order. The moss garden from the "Saiho-ji" Temple and the garden from the "Shugakuin" Detached Palace with its lush green rolling hills, are yet another expression of the Japanese reverence and religious feeling for the landscape.

In the Western World, on the other hand, the Renaissance brought a secular emphasis to the garden and produced the glorious examples of Italy, France and England — Villa Lante, Villa d'Este, Boboli Gardens, Versailles, Villandry, St. James, Hampton Court, Chiswick House. These, for the most part, were pleasure gardens for the wealthy. One wonders if perhaps our Judeo-Christian belief in the evils of the Garden of Eden might have delayed our development of, and enjoyment of, garden spaces. For example, it was not until the nineteenth century that community planning and garden and open spaces as part of the life of the common man really came into its own.

OUR RIGHT TO OPEN SPACE, BEAUTY AND PEACE

Today, in the last decade of the twentieth century, through a great deal of study and research, we are finally able to embrace the concept that mankind needs green spaces, open spaces, playgrounds and public areas, both physiologically and psychologically. Individuals need spaces in which to interact with each other and ameliorate their isolation. Beyond that, people need to counteract the effects of industrialization and expanding populations. They need to conserve their national parks and the geographic wonders that make our planet a wondrous place.

In the urban environment, we also need plants to counteract smog, to allow us places for meditation and give us islands of serenity in the morass of chaos. We need open spaces to counteract crowding and remind us of our humanity. We need a way to return to our pastoral roots and once again make contact with the earth. It was the earth, after all, that gave us nourishment and sustenance in the beginning. Before technology. Before urbanization.

How we accomplish this, and provide natural, open, serene spaces for our population is very much an expression of the values we cherish at this moment in time. The year 2,000 looms as a momentous turning point, a pivot, a way into an unimaginable future. Throughout this book we will illustrate the ways in which many designers view, and have viewed, the last twenty and perhaps the next hundreds of years. Each design is unique in its concept and execution. Consciously or sub-consciously, each designer probably envisioned this expression as a way to improve both the present state of the earth and the future. Certainly they viewed their solutions as a way to promote a more orderly, more beautiful, sane environment.

CHAPTER I

Private Spaces

A Luxury or a Necessity?

With the growth of the population behind the fortified enclosure, open spaces disappear, the irregular interstices between the single houses are filled by an agglomeration of other buildings, the thoroughfares are reduced to a minimum, and only narrow lanes and dead-end alleys are left to provide access to most houses. Rounded corners often ease the confined flow of traffic. Nowhere is any room left for gardens or green areas.

Cities and Planning in the Ancient Near East
Paul Lampl; George Braziller, New York 1968

From this quotation one might deduce that to provide private spaces, gardens, open spaces, green areas for the average inhabitant of a city in the Ancient Near East was not of prime importance. One might also consider, at the same time, that to provide private spaces, gardens, open spaces, green areas is not of prime importance for the average inhabitant of today's city — in any part of the world.

That's not to say that such spaces do not exist in the city structure of today's "fortified enclosures," today's urban environments. But for the most part, these so-called "private spaces," the Individual Gardens, the Estate Gardens, the Rooftop Gardens & Playgrounds, the Gardens for Multiple Dwellings and the Hotel & Resort Grounds are not accessible to all the inhabitants of a city.

In a small town, this may not be true. The majority of the inhabitants may own, or have access to front yards, backyards, open countrysides, and the like. But when discussing private spaces in most urban environments, one must be aware of the cost of land, and the fact that the average family cannot afford the luxury of using space just to provide a place to grow plants, have a play space or simply place to escape the tumult, noise and chaos of urban life. The economics of space, as opposed to the need for space, sunlight, quiet and privacy as these aspects of living affect health and quality of life, is an issue that we are just beginning to deal with.

SPACE & THE QUALITY OF LIFE

Adequate space, privacy, and the time to use these chosen places for meditation and communion either with oneself or one's fellow human beings is (according to most anthropological and psychological studies) a basic human need. The satisfaction of this need brings out the best in people and in their relationships with others; the denial of this need often brings out the worst in human behavior. If, indeed, one of the goals of the art of landscape design is to improve the quality of life, uplift the human spirit and expand the individual's vision and sense of self, then space and privacy are certainly

elements that contribute to these goals. But not always in the same way for different sites, clients, qualities of life — and, of course, different cultures.

To begin to understand what import these statements have on how, when and in what way one uses various design elements, specific materials, it would be well to briefly examine, for example, how each of these separate design categories — Individual Gardens, Estate Gardens, Rooftop Gardens & Playgrounds, Gardens for Multiple Dwellings, Hotel & Resort Grounds — might differ from each other in execution, goals and the enhancement of life that they offer.

INDIVIDUAL GARDENS — The Private Oasis

Two elements are possibly responsible for the average man's need to possess and inhabit a private garden space — an oasis. The first is the need to individuate oneself from one's parents and the world as a whole — to define oneself as an individual. The second is perhaps the desire to establish one's roots in a neighborhood, community, or country and contribute to the making of and continuity of that place. Perhaps that could be defined as a continuation of the process of individuation that leads eventually to the process of being a responsible and contributing member of society. Perhaps, then, psychological need leads into social awareness.

Throughout history, royalty and the wealthy classes created private gardens and oases for themselves. Hopefully, at the same time, they contributed something to the society that allowed the largess with which they designed and built these private horticultural wonders. In point of fact, some of these Estate Gardens are still being designed and built today, and this book includes samples of these designs. Other Estate Gardens of the past are also included in another category — Inspirational & Historic Spaces. The cost of maintaining the almost park-like estates of the past has dictated that what was once the domain of the wealthy has become accessible to the average man.

In the past, before the average man had access to the estate gardens, he could not hope to own a small plot of land for himself, he could not foresee a chance to arrange his own destiny, he could not begin to emulate the royal and wealthy, even in the smallest degree. Just to consider the concept of "arranging his own destiny," this "average man" had to have the time — the *leisure* time — to create this oasis. He also had to be free to use this land for the growing of beauty, not for the growing of food. Enter the "middle class."

In Europe, probably beginning in the seventeenth and eighteenth centuries, and, certainly, flowering in the middle of the nineteenth century with the Industrial Revolution, the mercantile classes, the entrepreneurs and the civil servants began to emerge, gain status, acquire small plots of land and have enough time (or enough servants) to create individual gardens. And were these just for their own enjoyment, their own quiet use? No. They were also to be shared and admired by all who saw them. They were hopefully — even the smallest plots — to be thought of as works of art. In cooperation with God and nature, of course.

The only problem with this paradigm is that it fits only the Western World and does not take into account the role that religion played, and still plays, in the creation of the gardens of the East — China, Korea and, especially, Japan. But perhaps in a perusal of the concept of the Oriental garden we can begin to understand some of the concepts needed for the design of gardens that are not just Individual Gardens, but gardens that allow privacy and shared spaces — Gardens for Multiple Dwellings and Hotel & Resort Grounds.

PRIVATE & SHARED — Open & Closed
The animist religion of the Chinese was responsible, in large part, for the design focus of the Oriental garden. Seas, mountains, rivers, rocks, trees were considered to be the manifestation of spirits that inhabited the earth in conjunction with human beings. It being a crowded world, good manners toward both the human and natural world were considered a necessity. Combined with this, and perhaps an integral part of it, was the Chinese philosopher Lao-Tzu's philosophy that stressed the integration of man's rhythms with the rhythms of nature — contemplation, moderation, a quest for calm and quiet.

The result of these two influences working side by side was a type of garden that was not meant for a display of wealth or to impress anyone. This garden was meant for sharing. It encouraged friends to sit side by side sharing perceptions and vistas created for the appreciation of the natural environment. A perfect concept for those people who share so-called "private spaces."

For the most part, in Gardens for Multiple Dwellings, the inhabitants are sharing space by necessity rather than by choice. The complexes may be low-income housing, retirement communities or garden apartments. But many of the inhabitants of these structures feel that maintaining any modicum of privacy is difficult, at best. The creation of quiet contemplative spaces to share with one, or at most a few friends, in conjunction with open interactive spaces to share with many is necessary to provide the inhabitants with pride and a sense of self. Time is also a most important consideration in these spaces.

Finding leisure time was essential for the creation of the Individual Garden. In the Gardens for Multiple Dwellings, however, perhaps *filling* leisure time is an equally important concept. Certainly it is in the design of Hotel & Resort Grounds. If you stop and think about it, many of the same problems are addressed and resolved in planning Gardens for Multiple Dwellings and Hotel & Resort Grounds.

Hotel & Resort Grounds are designed primarily around activities for leisure time. But, at the same time, guests want a certain modicum of privacy and escape from noise on their vacations — time to refresh themselves and calm their souls. How do you arrange traffic to accommodate these conflicting needs? How do people pass from one activity to another without interfering in the activities or privacy of others? These are not always easy problems to solve, but they are problems which the examples shown have at least dealt with in some successful ways.

THE OVERALL CRITERIA
The overall concept that this chapter — Private Spaces — attempts to deal with, then, is the need for privacy — the need to commune with oneself and with nature, and the spaces and ways in which our inventive minds find to do just this. The examples chosen are different scales — some are large, some very small — in terms of the amount of space they encompass. There are also other criteria for selection: the availability of the site, for example.

In an urban environment, rooftops are a wonderful source of space and also an almost guaranteed example of a private area. Depending, of course, on where the neighboring buildings are and how much taller they are than your particular roof. But all things considered, more and more examples of rooftop gardens and playgrounds are being developed and used.

"Used" is the important word here. A private space, no matter how meticulously designed, how expertly installed, no matter how beautiful, is a failure if it is not used. By this I don't necessarily mean actively used. To sit and look at a beautiful space, to contemplate it, is to "use" it. This aspect of design is perhaps the grayest and most difficult of the design process.

The creation and execution of a successful design needs the input of both the designer and the client — a synthesis. The client has to articulate his or her needs and the designer has to listen. Neither is an easy process. Hopefully, the designs on the next pages are examples of a successful synthesis in many different situations, because each design process is a unique experience.

Creative Transitions

In the design of the *STUDIO GARDEN* for Ruth and Jeffrey Scheuer, Landscape architect *Signe Nielsen* accomplished two different types of transition. The first was the creation of a garden space that would allow the residents to "travel" from a living environment to a creative working environment — from house to studio. The second was the evolution of this historic site (the house dates from 1830) from the nineteenth to the twentieth century without sacrificing the character of the site or creating an environment inappropriate with the visual appearance of the structures.

The sense of movement from one structure to the other is accomplished both by creating different levels in the garden and by using a combination of rectangular and undulating forms to sinuously and angularly lead the inhabitant through a series of spatial experiences. In addition, the year-round fish pond ensconced in the free-form raised planter adds still another element of movement with both the water and the fish.

The lilac bluestone and purple Vermont slate used as paving, the brick planter and wall materials are in total harmony with the brick exterior of the converted carriage house and the original structure. In

contrast, the rhythm of the planting in the planters and pots provides a softness and lushness to the hard edges of these materials. By providing a lushness of plant materials along the edge of the pool, the clematis, wisteria and climbing rose on trellises and walls, the design creates a sense of privacy and isolation. The photographs express a space that could exist behind walls in the country as well as the city. The designer has seen to it that the city does not intrude.

The use of wooden garden furniture, carefully placed sculpture and the color of the flowering azaleas and rhododendron create almost a sense of a country garden in a very small (1,300 sq. ft.) space. In this oasis of stone and plants, hard edges and soft flowing vines and shrubs, natural and man-made materials, one has the sense of being able to work peacefully on creative endeavors in the old carriage house that has given way to studio space. Leisure time can be well used here.

Project
Studio Garden
Location
New York, New York, USA
Client
Jeffrey and Ruth Scheuer
Design Firm
Signe Nielsen
Photographers
Signe Nielsen, James Morse

Grass, Apples and Hay

An English Garden

When the apple trees flower, the grass is starred with those flowers which do succeed, and foaming masses of cow parsley reach head height, it is irresistibly lovely. Later, when the grass is dry and golden blond (in recent years we have not cut it until late August) it has an almost metallic texture, glinting in the sun. Finally, when we cut the hay, the whole scale and space of the orchard changes dramatically, and the swirling patterns of short rough grass and lawn provide us with interest throughout the winter. The trees, too, provide excellent crops of apples.

With these words, *Christopher Carter* of the Landscape Architectural firm of *Colvin and Moggridge* describes his own garden, in *ALVESCOT, ENGLAND*. This description evokes the beauty of the timeless cycles of nature and the seasons, the scents of flowers and mown hay, picking fruit and altogether enjoying the bounty and evolution of the natural environment. The sense of design which he has brought to this old orchard surrounded by fields, five kilometers from the River Thames, is one in which the existing plant materials and configurations have not been altered so much as enhanced by the new installations. Great

care has been exercised to maintain an ecological balance in both the plants and the land. From the beginning he was determined to retain the character of the orchard within a meadow.

The contrasts and rhythms of this garden are achieved by configuring the existing materials — in this case a multitude of grass. By mowing the grass and creating smooth and rough textures, the meadows take on a flowing character, much as a meandering river or stream.

Opposing materials are altogether absent. Most paving, houses (both walls and roofs), garden and field walls, and even gravel are composed of Cotswold oolitic limestone — a golden-grey color that contrasts with the lush green of the grass and shrubs.

Immediately surrounding the house the designer has created what he calls "small areas of intensive gardens" which serve to provide both a physical and visual separation from the vista of the more grand spaces of the orchard. In this, he has created the intimate spaces necessary for a feeling of containment and privacy, while at the same time providing space for a vegetable garden and defining the limits of the property.

The siting of a beehive within the apple orchard further enhances the sense of maintaining and perpetuating the best of the wealth of nature. Here one can spend leisure time contemplating the beauty and timelessness of nature while studying ways in which to maintain and nurture it.

Project
Designer's Own Garden
Location
Alvescot, Oxford, England
Client
Christopher and Stephanie Carter
Design Firm
Colvin and Moggridge
Landscape Architects
Christopher N. Carter, Stephanie Carter
Photographer
Christopher N. Carter

The "Green Vault"

In designing his own residence, *THE SANABRIA HOUSE, Eduardo J. Sanabria, Arquitecto,* had specific problems to solve. If he was going to enjoy the view (the house is situated at an altitude of 3,500 feet with the view toward the sunrise, wind and rain), he had to find a way to incorporate the view and yet screen out the elements. He solved this problem by a combination of planting and enclosures.

His first, short-term design solution was to place a glass wall across the whole width of the lot. This allowed the occupants to take advantage of the view and, at the same time, protected them from the rain and the wind. His long-term solution was to plant rain trees. He refers to these rain trees as a "green vault" over the outdoor space. As these trees have grown (they were planted over 20 years ago), Eduardo Sanabria feels that they

have succeeded in controlling the elements — wind, rain, sun — in successful ways.

This private residence also incorporates an indoor patio covered with a metal pergola, as well as an outdoor terrace. The paving of these two spaces is a contrast in scale and texture in much the same way the intimate planting contrasts with the scale of the view in the distance. In point of fact, there are many elements of contrast on this site, the most predominant of which might be the elements of light and dark, sunshine and shadow. Since Caracas is located 10 degrees north of the equator, sunlight comes both from the north and south. This intense light, playing in and out of the rain trees, the ferns,

palms, glass walls, pergolas and patios, creates exotic views in the near spaces as these spaces frame and focus on the distant vistas.

At the same time, however, the ability to watch the play of the cycles of nature as rain clouds form and the wind alters the mass, must be a spectacular by-product of this garden design. This concept of creating an intimate space that, as the designer describes it, "nature is busy improving," in order to contemplate the grand design of nature is perhaps one of the most important ways in which we can spend our leisure time. Certainly it is in keeping with the Chinese Taoist tradition of creating specific areas in a garden to sit and contemplate the vista with a friend.

Perhaps in this garden the unending cycles and the power of nature are what one might observe. On the other hand, one might just be conscious of the texture of the small paving stones in the interior patio and the play of light on the ferns.

Project
Sanabria House
Location
Caracas, Venezuela
Client
Eduardo J. Sanabria
Design Firm
Eduardo J. Sanabria, Arquitecto
Photographers
William Niño. Carlos Corbacho

Down to the Sea
in Steps

In designing the *HOUSE and GARDEN for OSVALDO BARZELATTO,* landscape architect *Marta Viveros Letelier* of the design firm *Marta Viveros - Arquitecto Paisajista* had to negotiate difficult grade levels and rocky cliffs to take the dwellers from the shelter to the shore. The site, a narrow strip of land approximately one-fourth as wide as it is deep, is situated on the coast of Chile in Balneario de Cachagua, about 150 kilometers north of Santiago. This location provides the owners with a small beach but a large and spectacular view of the Pacific Ocean.

A series of steps, walls and ramps lead down from the front of the property to the beach below. Using brick and concrete, as well as elements of the indigenous rocks, the designer leads you down in stages. To stop and appreciate the view while descending these stages, a gazebo has been placed at the top of the cliff, amid a cluster of rocks. The angularity of these stepped surfaces and retaining walls is in keeping with the jagged and rugged appearance of the natural rock forms which seem thrust and broken rather than sculpted and smoothed by the timeless motion of the sea. The planting, on the

other hand, seems softer and gentler, as if nature here was capable of two faces, two sides of one coin.

Using massed fuchsias, evergreens and other native planting materials, the hard edges of this environment are gently softened. In a sense, with the carefully placed sculpture and the somewhat traditional aspects of the design, the designer seems to be staking a claim for human civilization in the midst of wilderness. At the same time, however, the designer never tries to deny that the

wilderness, the cliffs, rocks and sea are the stronger force in this partnership.

In fact, all facets of this design point to this concept. The orientation of the plan, the terrace above, the gazebo and siting of the house, all focus on the sea — not just as beach for sunning and swimming, but as a source of calm and inspiration. The view is of primary importance in this plan. In many ways it seems difficult to call this installation a "garden." The entrance with the walls, the hanging plants, the civilized calmness, is a garden in the traditional sense. But as one descends from the civilized to the primeval, the sense of "garden" is replaced by a sense of the glory of the uncultivated natural spaces of the planet.

Project
Casa Osvaldo Barzelatto
Location
Balneario de Cachagua, Chile
Client
Osvaldo Barzelatto
Design Firm
Marta Viveros Arquitecto Paisajista
Architects
Fernando Arnello, Ignacio Varas
Photographers
Fernando Arnello R., Osvaldo Barzellato

Opposite Ends of the Spectrum

The design of a *PRIVATE RESIDENCE* in Lake Forest, Illinois, appears to be two opposed design styles situated at the two ends of rather long, narrow lot on top of a bluff overlooking the shores of Lake Michigan. On closer inspection, however, one can understand why *Joe Karr of Joseph Karr & Associates* has implemented the design elements in this way — the organic and informal as opposed to the formal.

The seemingly organic aspects of the entry court of the main house, for example, actually are organized around an existing bluestone, circular entry court — a formal element in itself. To complement this, the entry stairs were extended and framed with Japanese lilac trees. The new swimming pool was added — another rather formal rectangular element — and areas added to "enhance indoor-outdoor transitions." These areas include such elements as planting areas of rhododendron, hybrid rhododendron and Japanese andromeda used in beds of pachysandra groundcover. Spreading yews are also used along with a copse of

European larch. These areas, informal and loosely laid out, serve as a transition to the existing wooded area that takes up the central and major portion of the site.

At the opposite end of the site from the main house, the designer added a tennis court, a pergola and a formal garden around the gate house and the studio/guest house. Here the plantings and shelters are starkly geometric in contrast to the background of the indigenous wooded area. However, in this rigidity there is a great deal of creative thought in the use of land forms and spatial vistas.

The tennis court is set down into a depression, surrounded by high grass slopes to permit use of a lower than normal court fence. This particular arrangement also allows those in the pergola canopy a central vantage point

for the court. The fence is planted with arborvitae so that the fronds can grow through and hide it — a structured environment softened by natural elements.

The 350-foot pergola was intended to be the dominant element on this end of the property in much the same way the house is at the other end of the property. The designer seemed to feel that to integrate this collection of landscape fragments into a cohesive whole, unity could be achieved through structural shelter elements rather than through planting alone. In this type of landscape installation (one in which it is obvious that use of leisure time in many different aspects is to be accounted for and utilized), perhaps this is the proper solution. Certainly, the existing natural landscape of the bluff overlooking the lake and the interior, thick-wooded area have not suffered from the improvements and alterations to the site. In fact, perhaps the designers have even illustrated to the owners of the property how carefully they must conserve and preserve these natural elements for future generations.

Project
Private Residence
Location
Lake Forest, Illinois, USA
Design Firm
Joe Karr & Associates: Joe Karr, principal
Landscape Contractor
Synnestvedt Landscape Company
Photographer
Joe Karr

A Classic Example

The *KAISER CENTER ROOF GARDEN* in Oakland, California, is considered a classic roof garden design. Built in 1960 under somewhat difficult structural constraints, this garden has not only survived well, it has improved with the maturity of the plant materials and served both as an oasis for the office workers and an inspiration for designers. This three-acre roof over a five-story parking structure was designed by *Theodore Osmundson and David Arbegast of Osmundson & Staley (now Theodore Osmundson & Associates)* as a semi-public park.

All the elements of landscape design — earth, rock, water, plant materials, man-made materials — were used in this installation and, at first glance, it's extremely difficult to comprehend that this garden is not at ground level. The configuration of the materials also adds to this illusion. The curvilinear paths that lead the visitor around the pond, through the planed, paved and grassy areas invite contemplation, wandering and rest in the midst of a busy urban environment. In the distance, perhaps one can glimpse Lake Merritt, another masterpiece of landscape design.

In some ways, this roof garden seems to mimic the grander, adjacent lake and

park. One could almost say that this raised site is a private miniaturization of the surrounding landscaped area near the *KAISER CENTER.* And perhaps that's not a bad analogy. In miniaturization — e.g., bonsai trees — great care is taken to adjust the plant to the environment through the pruning and training of roots, etc. The word bonsai means "tray-planted." In a sense a roof garden is "tray-planted." On a much larger scale, of course.

The care the designers took in their installation, their large scale "tray-planting," was extremely complex. Special soils and additives had to be selected to reduce the weight and provide the proper drainage. Care had to be taken in the selection of trees to make sure the roots grew horizontally instead of vertically. Soil had to be deep enough for trees and yet shallow enough to reduce weight. The pond had to have a water supply and proper drainage. And yet the designers didn't want a garden that would express this technology. They were designing a natural environment with only one

difference: the subsoil was concrete and the entire area floated six stories above the ground.

After 31 years one might say they succeeded. Users still continue to pass peaceful minutes or hours here. Noise is reduced by being above ground, and nothing seems to be lost in terms of the beauty of the natural materials.

Project
Kaiser Center Roof Garden
Location
Oakland, California, USA
Client
Kaiser Center, Inc.
Design Firm
Theodore Osmundson & Associates, Landscape Architects
Designers
Theodore Osmundson, FASLA; David E. Arbegast, FASLA
Photographer
Theodore Osmundson
Consultants
George Bell & Associates, Inc., Irrigation Consultants; Scott Beamer & Associates, Electrical and Mechanical Engineers
Awards
ASLA Professional Award; Garden Clubs of California

Beyond the Classic
Innovative Techniques & Materials

David Arbegast who had worked on the Kaiser Center Roof Garden stated in 1978, "Nobody's come up with anything new in building roof gardens since we worked on the Kaiser Center." That may have been true until *Theodore Osmundson* of *Theodore Osmundson & Associates* began the research and design for the *KAISER RESOURCES LTD, ROOF GARDEN* in Vancouver, British Columbia. The structural constrictions on this building were complex and, at first, seemed

insoluble. But in the final design and installation, he solved the technical problems and, once again, succeeded in creating a natural environment poised above the earth — 18 stories above the earth.

This aerie, which Osmundson describes as "a combination of Japanese garden, California patio and the Trevi Fountain," had, besides structural problems, the problems of accessibility and circulation. In this solution, the visitor goes from jewel to jewel along the narrow corridor-like roof garden. In each of the separate areas, the view from one to the other invites the user to move on and explore. In addition, the magnificent panoramas of the natural landscape are a backdrop and foil for the installation.

Plastics (Grass-Cel subsurface drainage medium, Metro-Media soil mix, fiberglass copies of rocks) and aluminum helped to reduce the load on the roof and allowed the designers to create a luxurious green

space with a pond, grass and colorful flower-filled planters. In this case, the technology was so well thought out and so carefully placed, that the installation seems

an extension of the area around Vancouver.

In many ways perhaps the three design influences — Japanese, Californian, Italian

— also reflect the past and present cultural heritage of Vancouver. Many immigrant peoples came to the West Coast to make up the populations, and it seems fitting that a garden design that surveys that landscape perhaps reflects what makes up the population of that landscape.

Project
Kaiser Resources Ltd., Roof Garden
Location
Vancouver, British Columbia, Canada
Client
Edgar F. Kaiser, Jr.
Design Firm
Theodore Osmundson & Associates, Landscape
Architects: design by Theodore and Gordon
Osmundson
Photographer
Theodore Osmundson
Consultants
George Bell Associates, Irrigation Consultants;
di Giacomo, Inc., Rockwork Specialists

The Nature of Retirement

The *MT. KONOCTI VILLAGE RETIREMENT COMMUNITY* offers lakeside living in community with the natural environment. The designers of *Tito Patri & Associates* undertook all the analytic functions of the design process — environmental analysis, capability zonation, ground water drainage problems, site planning, and, in the process, achieved an installation that integrates the natural elements of the site into the design solution.

This ninety-acre development near Clear Lake, Lake County, California, has been conceived and laid out to meet the needs of a retirement community — a group of residents with an ample amount of leisure time. The design considerations of this type of residential community are, in many ways, unique. For example, recreation areas for senior citizens have different criteria than recreation areas for children, or teenagers or active adults.

How do you design spaces that will work for this type of community?

The designers of this project achieved a balance of areas by using the natural slope of the site as one way of differentiating areas. Using stepped areas around open courts creates, for example, an area for meeting, playing games or performing. The steps can become seating. A small amphitheater is created. But always in keeping with the natural environment.

Natural materials were incorporated throughout the site. The plant materials — redbud, arctostaphylos, ceanothus, oak, bay, tanbark oak, madrone, digger pine, toyon, huckleberry — all are native to northern California, and the large boulders used throughout, were uncovered during the grading of the site.

This complex, which includes both outdoor recreation areas and a community

center has been designed for people to sit in the sun, wander the paths, meet and chat with each other in the privacy of community. Here the residents are not at the mercy of the stress of the urban environment. Here the environment is one of peace and enjoyment of nature. In point of fact, this entire design appears at peace with itself and with the natural landscape.

Project
Lakeside Haven
Location
Konocti Harbor, Lakeport, Lake County, California, USA
Client
Plumbers Union (San Francisco Locals)
Design Firm
Tito Patri & Associates
Landscape Architect
Tito Patri, FASLA
Project Designer
Edward Janelli
Architect
Robert Herman
Photographer
Tito Patri

Roof Gardens, Ponds & Pavilions

The *VILLA SASSA* in Lugano, Switzerland, is designed with a formality to the plan and a playfulness in the execution. In this "Senior Residence" and hotel, the designers of *Studio Heiner Rodel* have created a peaceful environment in which one might retire and, at the same time, they've created an interplay of spaces that promote fantasy and childhood delight.

By restoring the old Villa Luvini and integrating it into the complex through the north/south axis, the environment achieves the feeling of a small city that has grown and been maintained over the years. In that sense — maintenance of the old being part of the growth of the new — perhaps it adds to the idea of spending

one's last years in the area. The mild and almost Mediterranean climate also enforces this idea. To take advantage of this benign atmosphere, the designers have used intensive Mediterranean planting materials. The look, the feel of the buildings is also Mediterranean. Even though the view over Lake Lugano to the mountains constantly reminds both the residents and the visitors that they are, indeed, in Switzerland, this micro-climate in which they exist belies the fact.

The paving materials, however, are indigenous granite slabs from local quarries,

even though the white carrara marble used in the fountains again takes us back to a Mediterranean influence. And the playful elements in the overall design of this project? Where does the cultural influence for these come from? Perhaps from the mind of the landscape architect and sculptor who created them, *Ivan Pestalozzi.*

In the wind-sculptures on the roof garden, the sculptor has used one of the most dynamic of the natural elements to achieve his design — the wind. Color also plays an important part in this installation. The bright colors of these moving abstract forms playing off one against the other have a sense of playful elegance against the calm white marble and stately composure of this protected hillside where one can spend one's later years in a peaceful setting.

Project
Villa Sassa
Location
Lugano, Switzerland
Client
Alpha Ltd.
Design Firm
Studio Heiner Rodel
Sculptor
Ivan Pestalozzi
Photographer
Buhler Karl-Dietrich

Rain Forests & the Coral Sea

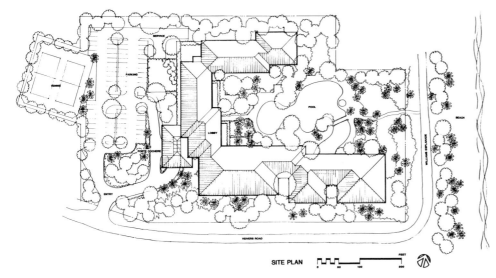

SITE PLAN

... all man-made elements were subordinate to the natural characteristics dominating the landscape. The different use areas were designed to complement and enhance the existing vegetation and no attempt was made to introduce artificial elements or 'features' which would detract from the overall magnificence of the site's natural assets. In this matter conservation of the area's great natural wealth and beauty was achieved together with the development of a prestigious international class tourist resort.

With these words, *Eugene Herbert of Siteplan,* a consultant on the *RAMADA REEF RESORT,* gives his accolades to *Wimberly, Allison Tong & Goo,* the architects for the project. The site, Palm Cove, on the Coral Sea in Cairns, Queensland, Australia, was an interdunal

paperbark swamp. The huge trees that dominated the site — *Melaleuca leucadendrons* — were not only saved in the resulting design, they were made an important design feature. The architects went so far as to create exposed concrete piers of fiberglass molds made from actual tree trunks. The architecture of the entire U-shaped building is a style that blends into the natural environment rather than dominating it. And the footprint of the entire hotel was designed to fit in and around and "accept" the largest of the *melaleucas*.

The swampy site also had certain technical problems — e.g., drainage. Since the site was in a cyclone prone area, one portion of the swamp was deepened and four large submersible pumps installed. These were screened from view with a pergola and trained climbing vines. Other recreational areas were added to take advantage of the natural site: sunken bar plaza; undercroft children's play area; turfed forecourt; children's sand play with a log play sculpture; hammock area; tropical fruit garden; outdoor coffee plaza; pre-conference deck. In each of these areas the natural vegetation and the contours of the land were taken into consideration and used to advantage. Except perhaps in the perimeter of the site.

To meet the pool safety requirements of the local authorities, the site had to be enclosed. The solution was to install a fence of vertical pine logs — a barricade. However, to keep this fence form feeling like a barricade, the earth was mounded from the inside up to the top of the fence, achieving privacy and enclosure without the psychological feeling of a barrier. The guests can stand at the top of the enclosure, on the earth mound, and gaze out at the Coral Sea. Yet another way to provide the necessities and still preserve the natural beauty of the site.

Perhaps the way the architects describe

the design and installation of the pool sums up their solution: "The large free-form Ramada Reef Resort pool, which weaves among a splendid grove of ancient *melaleuca* trees, was built above ground to avoid damage to the trees' root system." Throughout this project all the members of the project team seem to have been almost awed by the presence of these

magnificent trees. This may represent landscape design at its best — finding ways to allow the human inhabitants of our planet to work and live in concert with the irreplaceable natural elements.

Project
Ramada Reef Resort
Location
Palm Cove, Cairns, Queensland, Australia
Client
International Resorts (Australia) Pty. Ltd.
Design Firms
Wimberly, Allison, Tong & Goo, Architects and Planners; Belt Collins & Associates Engineering Planning and Landscape Architecture
Landscape Architect
Siteplan
Photographers
David Franzen, WAT & G, Monte Costa,
Jon Ivanovic - Studio One

CHAPTER II

Interactive Spaces

A Sharing of Needs

The term, "Interactive Spaces" might also be defined as "a void between opposing solids," in that it encompasses those spaces that are not really private, but, on the other hand, are not public spaces either. In some instances there are elements of exclusivity in these spaces. For example, in corporate complexes, one might be able to see the grounds and plazas but be unable to enter them because of security considerations. Other spaces might be accessible for a fee, or by passing through barriers and other protective mechanisms. In all cases, however, one cannot really define these spaces as either strictly Private Spaces or Public Spaces.

To further clarify the issue, it's also important to understand that these spaces are maintained primarily by private funds — corporations, foundations, educational institutions and the like. In spite of the private support and maintenance for these spaces, the concept behind them is surprisingly similar — a desire to allow individuals space in which to alleviate their alienation by contact with other human beings, while at the same time communing with nature, either in controlled man-made environments that showcase increments of nature, or in man-made structures that allow views of those areas of untouched, primal wilderness that still exist in the midst of our constant cultivation of the land.

ALIENATION & INTERACTION
Alienation, that inability to communicate with and care about other human beings, that feeling of being an outsider, of not belonging, may or may not be caused by living in an urban environment. But most experts would agree that living in an urban environment might exacerbate the condition. Can anything be done about it? Perhaps providing more spaces, such

as in these examples on the following pages, is one small step in solving the problem.

"Time" is a vital ingredient in the development of Interactive Spaces. Whereas leisure time was something to be *desired* in order to create Private Spaces, leisure time is something to be *filled* in Interactive Spaces. As you peruse the following pages and contemplate how the designers have solved the problems inherent in creating these spaces — Atriums & Indoor Gardens, Corporate & Industrial Complexes, Sports & Games Complexes, Civic, Cultural & Nature Centers, Campus Grounds & Masterplans — keep in mind that each of these examples has a common goal: to provide a place to interact with both nature and man in a way of individual choosing, as a participant or an observer, but always during one's *leisure* time. To help illustrate this concept of interaction let's explore some of the different forms these examples take.

THE OUTDOORS INDOORS
One of the more interesting spaces to be embraced by designers in the last 20 years is the Atrium & Indoor Garden. Corporations have created indoor plazas, suburban malls and other retail establishments have used atrium spaces as marketing tools, and various other building types have employed this device as a way to bring both light and plant materials into interior spaces. Many years ago Buckminster Fuller proposed enclosing cities with massive geodesic domes to control climate and pollution. Perhaps atrium spaces are a first small step in realizing that concept.

The control of climate is a primary factor in the creation of these spaces. In cold, wet climates, they provide shelter and a sense of life — green spaces, flowers — during the long winter months. In hot climates, heavily planted, shady indoor atrium spaces can provide a respite from a hot unrelenting sun. Climate control is crucial at both extremes.

There is also another more esoteric service that the Atrium & Indoor Gardens can provide — a giant greenhouse, a place to propagate, experience and enjoy exotic plant life from around the world. This idea was very popular during the Victorian Era, and witnessing a garden of giant bamboo in the midst of an Eastern city on a winter day brings those memories to mind.

BEING THE "GOOD GUYS"
During the last 20 to 30 years there has been a great deal of negative publicity concerning the role corporations and industry have played in polluting the environment. Whether it is to overcome and undo this publicity, or whether they simply have learned better environmental practices, corporations now seem — if one can learn from the results of their building programs — to be concerned with building campuses, complexes, buildings and plazas, if not in harmony with the environment, then at least not opposed to, or in opposition to it. These examples show innovative and constructive use of the land, preservation of green and open spaces and creation of Sports & Games Complexes.

These Corporate & Industrial Complexes encompass sometimes hundreds of acres, preserving a great deal of the open space for future generations. That in itself is a major contribution of the corporations. But another important contribution becomes apparent as one studies the examples of Landscape Design over the past decades. Just as religious institutions supported artists in past centuries and gave them commissions as places to display their work and their talents, corporations now seem to be playing that role.

If you study many of the corporate plazas illustrated, you'll see the work of sculptors and other artists, as well as the work of landscape designers. It seems to be a happy marriage. The marrying of the private individual into

the wilderness is perhaps a more tentative partnership and one that requires a bit more care.

THAT DELICATE BALANCE
To achieve this partnership that allows us to enter into the carefully preserved wilderness or natural environment requires a delicate touch. How do you provide human intrusion without allowing human intervention? The great caves of Lascaux finally had to be closed because of the damage done — not by intention or by vandalism — to those prehistoric images. Light, the air breathed by the thousands of visitors, perhaps even spores and dust from their clothing all contributed to the potential destruction. Now visitors are allowed only into a facsimile. And here we're discussing an inanimate environment. Consider the effects of human intrusion and intervention on a living environment.

One example of a rather unique type of conservation is illustrated on the following pages. Two designers poised the visitors over the natural preserve to allow them to see and be in the midst of this area, so to speak, but not really to set foot in it. Is this hovering technique something landscape designers should consider for the future? Certainly in this case it allows the visitors an educational experience without damaging the environment. And the last part of this chapter concerns educational experiences in the Campus Grounds & Masterplans developed by several different designers.

GROWTH & EDUCATION
Campus Grounds & Masterplans are very much what the title states. The primary focus of most of our examples, though, is on the integration of the new and the old — the growth of an educational complex and the ensuing problems, and sometimes benefits. There are many schools of thought on masterplans and their efficacy. Should a campus by totally planned from inception with no allowance for future growth? That's a stable concept but not a very practical one.

Learning and knowledge, like plant life, don't seem to stop growing.

Tomorrow there will be new discoveries, new knowledge and new ways of teaching. To accommodate these changes, new structures and spaces may have to be designed and built. Any successful master planning has to encompass these new areas and needs. How? Well, of course, that is the problem of the campus today. To sacrifice the old and historic to make way for the new, to lose the sense of history and time that the buildings on a campus embody, seems shortsighted. But perhaps there are no perfect solutions. Land is not in unlimited supply.

AN UNLIMITED SUPPLY OF TIME
Time also is not in unlimited supply, although we are promised every year that the future will give us more and more time to ourselves. If we had more time, how would we spend it?

Time without purpose is empty time. The concept of this book is usable space, and time to enjoy that space. But these constructs must be balanced carefully if we are to enjoy our leisure and our Interactive Spaces. Perhaps some of these spaces should provide more in the way of activities for people. Or is that the purpose of Public Spaces? As in many areas, the categories imposed on the examples in this book are sometimes arbitary. Many times they overlap. As you study the examples on the following pages — Atriums & Indoor Gardens, Corporate & Industrial Complexes, Sports & Games Complexes, Civic, Cultural & Nature Centers, Campus Grounds & Masterplans — consider which of these examples with just a few changes could, and should, truly serve as Public Spaces?

An Oasis from the Storm

In non-moderate climates, the creation of an oasis allows the inhabitants to function well in extremes of temperature. In addition, an oasis brings to mind serenity, an escape from surrounding unpleasantness. Certainly, in urban environments an escape from surrounding unpleasantness is devoutly to be wished for. Another desirable concept is the idea of connection, both with places and with people. The WINTER GARDEN at the WORLD FINANCIAL CENTER seems to satisfy all these definitions of oasis. It protects the user from the heat and cold of the eastern United States, it provides an escape from the bustle and sometime squalor of the surrounding environment and it provides a meeting and connecting space.

The designer Diana Balmori, of Balmori Associates, was charged with the task of creating an indoor space to connect the World Financial Center with the World Trade Center and, in addition, to provide a meeting space that would serve up to 35,000 pedestrians per hour. Naturally, the space would protect the user from the elements, but could it, at the same time, take advantage of the panorama over the Hudson River, and the excitement of the interplay of the skyline of lower Manhattan? Perhaps a conventional space might not have succeeded in fulfilling all these needs, but this grand glass hall with the huge bay window that focuses attention on the Hudson is superb. One has a sense of never having left the outdoor spaces behind. The light from the vaulted hall, the open space with the interior grove of palm trees set in the paved marble floor give the impression of a Mediterranean space put down in the middle of the city to provide solace to the visitor on cold winter afternoons. Even the planting (*Washingtonia robusta* and *Washingtonia filifera*, both native to California), seems to indicate to the visitor that life and warmth exist, even on the coldest, bleakest days.

To further intensify this feeling of containment and oasis, the designers have created shops and restaurants on the periphery of the grand hall. Seating is provided by movable units which can be arranged and rearranged much in the same way as the grand squares of Europe. The grand staircase and the changes in level also contribute to this feeling of an old, timeless, grand public space.

The question of what constitutes a public space does arise, however. Is a space such as this, which has controlled access to some extent, truly a public space? Can anyone come in and use this space, or are there a set of unwritten rules that allow use only by those thought to be acceptable?

Project
Winter Garden Interior Landscape Design,
World Financial Center
Location
Battery Park City, New York, New York, USA
Client
Olympia & York
Design Firm
Cesar Pelli and Associates, Inc.; Diana Balmori,
interior landscape design; Cesar Pelli, building
design; Thomas Morton, project manager

Photographers
Robert Benson, Kenneth Champlin
Peter Mauss/Esto
Consultant
M. Paul Friedberg, associate landscape architect
Awards
1985 Certificate of Merit, The Municipal Arts
Society of New York; 1988 Best Project, Grand
Winner for the Winter Garden, Interiorscape
Magazine; 1990 Honor Award, Connecticut
Society of Architects

A Humanizing Element

The designers of the atrium space in *THE HARBORSIDE FINANCIAL CENTER,* architects *Beyer Blinder Belle* and landscape architects *Zion & Breen Associates,* wanted to create what they call a "humanizing element" in this vast commercial complex on the Husdon River in New Jersey. This entire development is slated to provide offices for more than 25,000 workers, plus homes for 1,500. Faced with the need to provide interactive space for more than 26,000 people each day, an atrium space was conceived as a contrast to the heavy masonry construction of this former "rail-to-keel" warehouse and exchange. In addition, this atrium space adds a light touch to the existing building, provides interior light, a meeting place and visual access to the waterfront.

By using this atrium as the main entrance to the complex and siting the atrium on an axis at right angles to the waterfront, the designers took advantage of the harbor view. They also created a

space that incorporates the natural elements of the waterside with the interior space by visually extending this view into the atrium. The space created by the atrium (a new space of steel and glass in opposition to the existing concrete and masonry) has been sensitively articulated to echo the rhythms of the existing exterior. The paving patterns, the different levels and transitions that open onto the retail areas are all configures geometrically. The brick paving, the glazing of the roof and the interior planters are solid in feeling, yet in their design they convey a sense of the lightness of this semi-transparent space.

The plant materials take this theme of solidity and yet lightness even further. The

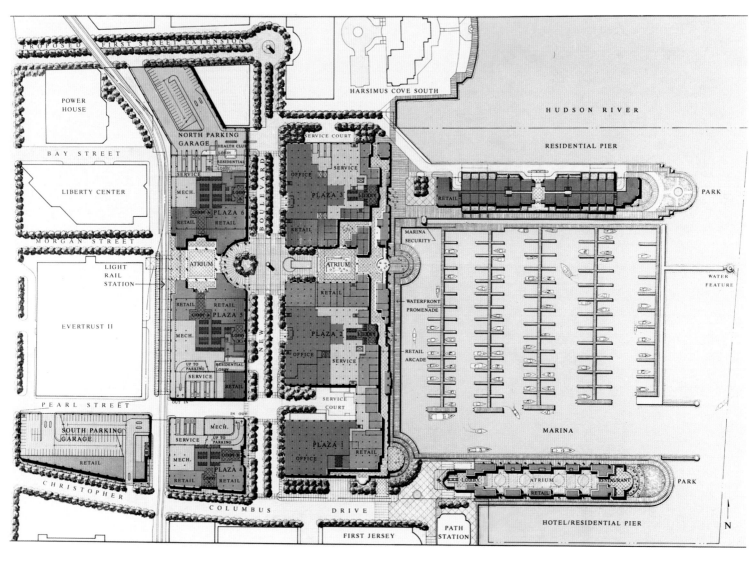

solid massing of the evergreen ground ascends upward into the lacy branches of bamboo that create gentle, intricate and changing patterns as the light changes. The light is, indeed, one of the delightful aspects of this interior space. The changing colors and shadow patterns provide accent and contrast and further define the different areas of this space.

This former service area has been transformed from a redundant space to a climate controlled area where office

workers can relax in inclement weather,
meet friends and attend formal functions.
By creating a space that incorporates
these activities, the designers have truly
created an area for interaction. Workers
and dwellers have a space to find shelter,
meet friends and engage in those "human"
activities that reduce stress and enhance
the day to day activities of urban life.

Project
Harborside Financial Center
Location
Jersey City, New Jersey, USA
Client
Jones Lang Wooten USA
Design Firm
Beyer Blinder Belle: John H. Beyer, partner-in-charge; Richard Visconti, base building; Chris Barriscale, project designer; Cameron Rashiti, project manager; Timothy Allenbrook, project manager, master plan; Ilan Tavor, construction administration; Robert McMillan, project architect
Landscape Architects
Zion & Breen Associates
Photographers
Peter Aaron/ESTO; Anne Edris
Awards
1990 Modernization Award, Buildings Magazine; 1990 New Good Neighbor Award, New Jersey Business and Industrial Association; 1987 Outstanding Non-Residential Award, American Planning Association, New Jersey Chapter

Stone Gardens in the Twentieth Century

It's evident from observing *Kisho Kurokawa's YASUDA FIRE INSURANCE BUILDING, FUKUOKA,* that the designers understand the subtle relationships between interior and exterior spaces. The unification of the outside and inside spaces, of course, has its origins in traditional Japanese architecture. One might also say that the sloping glass facade encapsulates the outside "stone garden" and brings it into the inside lobby. This use of reflection to define space plays against the hard edges and lines of the exterior space. This exterior space is, in itself, yet another expression both of the historical/cultural influences in Japan and of the international sociological/technological influences. For example, to use a historical concept such as a "stone garden" defines this corporate plaza/office building lobby as indigenous to Japan. To use contemporary high-tech

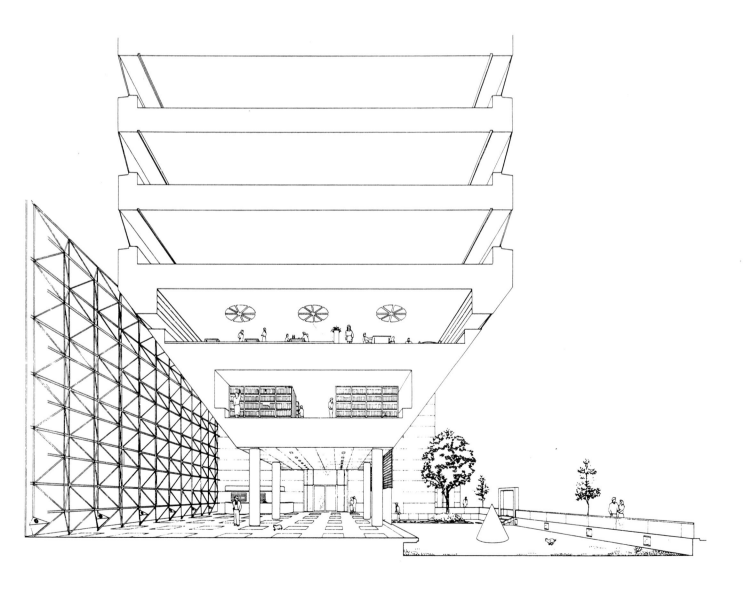

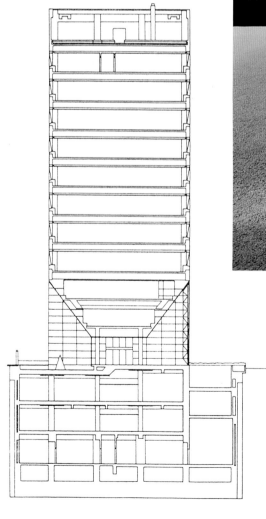

materials to execute this concept defines this design as done in the latter part of the twentieth century, in a milieu of international trade and cooperation. It also expresses the technological expertise of Japanese society and Japanese designers.

The forms in the garden, reminiscent of rock and stone shapes, with their hard, sleek edges contrasted against the raked stone of the plaza with the minimum planting, may also be a profound expression of our twentieth-century dilemma. Are we so reluctant to provide green spaces in our urban environment that we carefully select plants as ornamental items to be enshrined as sculpture? Are these plants becoming icons to a past that we dimly remember — a past that provided green spaces and natural areas where we could rest, meditate and restore our battered lungs and psyches?

Overall, this example of urban corporate landscaping is a restful oasis. But one or two trees are not a replacement for the peace, beauty and tranquility of a forest. However, one must be aware that the problem of pollution could counterbalance the need and desire for extensive planting materials. Perhaps it's difficult to get plants to grow in this urban area. On the other hand, plants can provide oxygen through photosynthesis — a product necessary for our survival.

Project
Stone Garden, Yasuda Fire Insurance Building
Location
Tokyo, Japan
Design Firm
Kisho Kurokawa Architects & Associates
Principal
Kisho Kurokawa
Photographer
Tomio Ohashi

Seasons and the Golden Mean

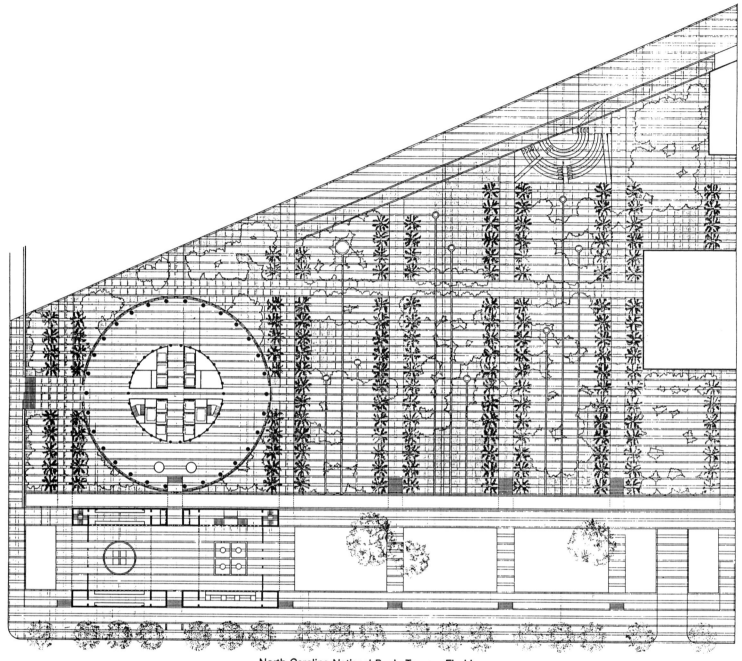

North Carolina National Bank, Tampa, Florida

Using the proportions of the "Golden Mean" and the Fibonacci series of logarithmic patterns to establish the grid system of the design concept, the *Office of Dan Kiley* designed an urban plaza adjacent to the North Carolina National Bank in Tampa, Florida, (designed by the architectural firm of *Wolf Associates*) that has become Tampa's first authentic urban park. According to Dan Kiley, the design process was essentially an attempt to "release people into space." Instead of just sculpting random spaces and letting the visitor roam unheeded through the spaces, this design takes the visitor and orients him or her through carefully articulated patterns and pathways of growing things and flowing things — plants and water — to the wonders and delights of a formal garden space executed in a contemporary manner.

The canals and pools of this grid pattern of grass and pre-cast concrete shapes are a light and silvery element that weaves through the carefully thought out arrangement to achieve a unity and clarity of design that is soothing in the manner of the best of the formal gardens. Here the landscape in not left just to change and nature to form and organize the plant materials. The other side of this, though, is the plant materials that Dan Kiley has chosen.

In the *NORTH CAROLINA NATIONAL BANK PLAZA*, seasons have been introduced alongside native, indigenous, evergreen plant materials. By using crape myrtle trees which shed their leaves, lie dormant and bud in the spring in a random pattern, played against the sabal palemettos in a geometric pattern, he has shown both the delight of the natural cycles of nature and the seasons, and the continuity and strength of the familiar indigenous plantings.

Other excitements of this installation are the multiple levels of this site. The upper and lower levels are separate but connected. The long terrace, the lower level and urban portion, acts as a visual focus. The upper level is raised eight feet above the ground to be invisible from the

street and in it is a green space, a garden private from the cityscape, in a way. Planting in the geometric patterns, even randomly, helps to divide this area into the different uses, such as the amphitheater and reflecting pool, which were designed by *Wolf Associates*.

From the random deliberateness of the planting, to the glass bottom canals lit from underneath by the parking garage, this thoughtfully articulated space has the character both of a delightful small city that has evolved over time and also of a gorgeous Persian miniature carefully articulated with symbolic elements, timeless in their ancient heritage.

Project
North Carolina National Bank Plaza
Location
Tampa, Florida, USA
Client
North Carolina National Bank
Architect
Wolf Associates: Harry Wolf, principal
Landscape Architect
Office of Dan Kiley
Photographer
Aaron Kiley

Renaissance Revisited

Dan Kiley says of FOUNTAIN PLACE, "The environment where people work should have gardens because it improves their sensibility, the morale and their imagination. Basically, it just makes them happy to be in that place versus some other place." Clearly, this interplay of calm, dark water and sparkling, dancing fountains would make people happy — especially in this hot, inland Texas city. An oasis in the desert is always welcome. This oasis with its geometric configurations, soldierly rows of trees and angular walks, not only complements these sleek, glass-skinned towers that rise like

diamond-cut stalagmites from the plaza, but also creates the real entrance lobby to the building. Designing a space that is a cross somewhere between a public park and a pond, Dan Kiley allowed this "plaza" to become a part of the structure, not just a green backdrop for the building.

It is said that this six-acre corporate plaza, with its four acres of water gardens covering over 70 percent of the site, is the most extensive water garden constructed since the Renaissance. In many ways the idea of renaissance, re-birth, humanistic revival of the arts, is a good analogy for this urban space. Instead of just creating a hot, dusty plaza in the traditional sense, Dan Kiley was intent upon creating a human space to delight the imagination and refresh the spirit. In this instance, he used water as the main design element.

The 400 bald cypress trees (each from an individual granite planter flush with the water level or the paving) provide a canopy over the ponds that changes with the seasons, providing shade, views in every direction and creating continuous surprises and changes. Two hundred sixty-three bubbler fountains in staggered rows are situated between the trees, giving this space the added excitement of the play of

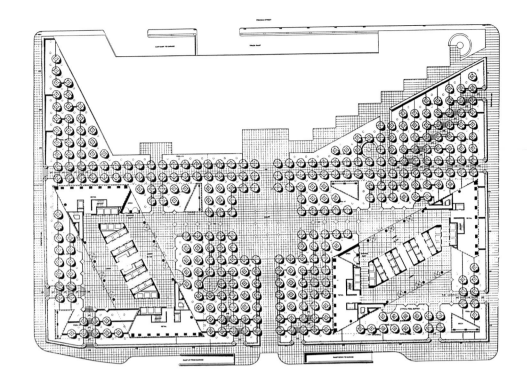

water. Water also laps onto the black and green slate paving, giving the whole area a wet, cool ambience.

The central fountain provides the focal element of surprise and change. It dominates the center of the plaza with its ever changing 160 fountain jets, programmed by computer to rise and fall in a seemingly random display of rising and falling water showers. This pièce de résistance is actually equipped with wind sensors that adjust the height to avoid excess sprays. Charm, delight and practicality are integrally designed both to enchant and protect the visitor.

With its variety of sensory experiences and its feeling of oasis and calm, this formal, ordered space, with its waterfalls and fountains under the roof of lacy trees, provides a space not only to interact, but to revel in the beauty of those natural elements so essential to human survival.

Project
Fountain Place
Location
Allied Bank Tower, Dallas, Texas, USA
Client
Criswell Development Company
Architects
I.M. Pei and Partners,
Harry Weese and Associates
Photographers
Aaron Kiley, Wes Thompson
Awards
1987 ASLA Merit Award

A Crack in the Earth

George Hargreaves created a man-made fissure in the earth, with mist machines hissing in the crack, as a symbolic "fountain" in *CHARLESTON PLACE*, a corporate complex in Mountain View, California. This "crack," this element, is meant to be an abstraction of the San Francisco Bay mud on which this project stands. George Hargreaves uses this form to represent the mud which forms fissures as it dries. He also wants to hint at aquifers deep within the ground at the bottom of the fissure. To enhance this illusion, the hand-sculpted concrete walls of the fissure are integrally colored to match the color of the bay mud.

This four-building office and research development complex cover 16.6 acres which the designer sculpted with a clean and spare hand. Natural materials are the building blocks for this design. The green of the lawn and jasmine groundcover, the sequoia and sycamore trees contrast with

the slick, hard materials of the geometrical building block and the stark white concrete of the pedestrian ways. An eight-hundred-foot long pedestrian path provides the central organizational element of the plan. At each end of this path, a major piece of public art has been installed. Across this central path, the pedestrian movement as a whole is designed on the diagonal, with a series of open spaces or "courtyards" throughout the site. This diagonal counter thrust is emphasized by the fissured "fountain" that links the courtyards and provides a connecting element to the design.

A wooded easement surrounds this site, giving a rural quality to the installation. This rural or agrarian (this once was farmland) quality is further enhanced in the parking lots. These are conceived as the "orchards" with trees planted in a grid pattern. Clipped hedges surrounding the square courtyards echo this geometric grid pattern which complements the structures on the site. The elegance of this

deceivingly simple design solution is in keeping with the theme of the complex — research and development. The illusion of things unseen, searched for, and yet essentially whole, natural and complete, is perhaps the principal of true research. And in his search for design solutions using earth forms and plant materials as his tools, George Hargreaves unearths new and hidden meanings in his final form.

Project
Charleston Place
Location
Mountain View, California, USA
Client
Mozart Development
Design Firm
Hargreaves Associates: George Hargreaves, principal
Photographer
Hargreaves Associates
Awards
1988 The Grand Award Pacific Coast Builders
Photographer
Hargreaves Associates

Floating Spheres & Time Machines

Heiner Rodel had a two-fold goal to achieve in the design of the courtyard of the *UBS ADMINISTRATION BUILDING* — he wanted to create a new entrance to the building and, at the same time, he wanted to create a recreational space for the employees. Also, he wanted to do this on a site in an industrial area crossed by heavy traffic and a railway line with two trains each day. Not an easy task.

The result is a space of different levels, with planting trees and pools interspersed throughout this geometric arrangement. There are some spaceframe shelters near the entrance, and to focus attention and create a sense of whimsy and humor there is a 12-meter high sculpture of filigree iron — the "Time Machine."

This delightful piece by the sculptor Ivan Pestalozzi is actually a working clock of sorts (as long as you don't need minutes and seconds). Every hour a colored polyester sphere drops into the two connecting ponds at the base of the

sculpture. Time is finite and recognizable. In contrast (and perhaps for emphasis) this wedge-shaped plaza is rather formal and contained in its design.

The design of the paving follows the geometry of the pools and planted areas, with light colored granite used for the linear framework and stairs. Inside this linear framework, porphyry cobblestone is used to give texture and a certain scale to sculpture. But even in this formality there is humor and a sense of play — for example in the choice of tree shapes and foliage. The trees (*Robinia pseudoaccacia "umbraculifera," Tilia cordata, Quercus robur "fastigiata"*) for the most part have

rounded shapes that echo the colored
spheres, and at times, look like all-day
suckers on a stick. Is this deliberate? One
can't know, of course, but joy, whimsy
and humor do seem to radiate out of this
installation. Perhaps the designer wanted
to counteract the noise and chaos of the
industrial site by instituting a playful note.
In this he succeeded.

Project
UBS Administration Building
Location
Zurich, Switzerland
Client
Union Bank of Switzerland
Design Firm
Studio Heiner Rodel
Sculptor
Ivan Pestalozzi
Photographer
Buehler Karl-Dietrich

From Rubble to Recreation

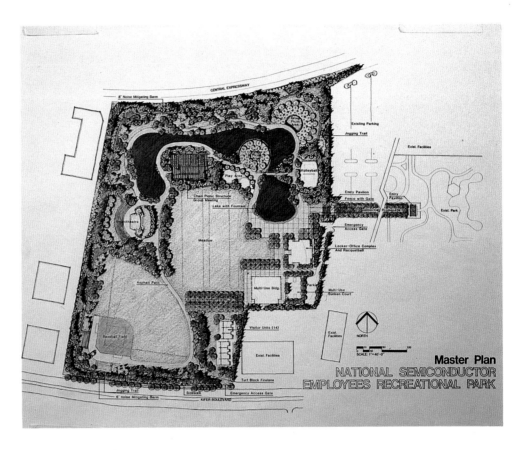

Master Plan
NATIONAL SEMICONDUCTOR
EMPLOYEES RECREATIONAL PARK

This delightful, well-used park and recreation area — the *NATIONAL SEMICONDUCTOR EMPLOYEES RECREATIONAL PARK* — was once a rubble-strewn field, a dump. All it took to transform this area was National Semiconductor's corporate president's resolve to create a "significant place" for employees, and the design talents of *Harold N. Kobayashi* of *Royston, Hanamoto, Alley & Abey.* The program for this park included creating a space that would serve to enhance morale and corporate unity and, at the same time, would be a park that employees would think of as their own. Naturally, this space would have to accommodate large-scale corporate events, but the president and the

designer also wanted the park to incorporate lunchtime use, family picnics, departmental and corporate games.

Using both natural and man-made materials, the designers developed a large-scale theme to transform the site. Eight-foot-tall enclosing berms were constructed at the perimeter of the site to mask the wind and highway noise, and a 1.5 acre lake plus a 1,000 seat amphitheater were added. The central meadow was created for soccer games and large gatherings (art shows, food tents, character races) and additional areas added for ball fields and volleyball. All of these areas exist in harmony, their individual activity nodes arranged within tree masses which define the spaces.

The approach to the park (a five-minute walk) is along a major promenade from the Fabrication Building through stone piers. A black metal arbor gate defines the

entrance and establishes the park motif —
an expression of the industrial nature of the
corporate complex. To further express this
motif, Harold Kobayashi designed the
park centerpiece of chain-link fabric. This
five-story-tall chain-link sculpture/shelter
resembling a giant tent serves not only a
practical function, it also gives an identity
both to the site and to the employees using
the site. The employees' identification with
this sculpture and the site is evident in the
numbers using the space. Use has
increased at the rate of 30 percent to 50
percent each year. Ten football teams, 40
softball teams, 12 soccer teams and 6

volleyball teams make the park their home.
    Employees also use the area to sit on
the berm and sunbathe or walk by the
lake. Both active and passive recreational
needs have been met by the corporation
and the designer. The designer refers to
the area as "the 'greening' of a hard and
unattractive environment." The instigators
and the creators have gone beyond
greening, however. From the innovative
idea of burying of the rubble inside the

berm, to the use of metal to reflect high
technology and stone to indicate the
timelessness, all those involved in the
creation of this space have been
responsible for building an oasis of both
the body and the spirit.

National Semiconductor Employees Recreational
Park
Location
Santa Clara, California, USA
Client
National Semiconductor
Design Firm
Royston Hanamoto Alley & Abey, Landscape
Architects: Robert Royston, Harold Kobayashi,
principals
Photographer
Mark Schwartz
Awards
1990 and 1985 Merit Award, NCC/ASLA
(Northern California Chapter, American Society
of Landscape Architects)

An Olympic Legacy

O*LYMPIC PLAZA* in Calgary was designed by *M. Paul Friedberg* to be an Olympic facility (a place to present medals) and also as a municipal plaza for the citizens of the city. This municipal plaza was intended for performances and for ceremonial functions. By the time M. Paul Friedberg had completed his design, however, the space had assumed a great many more functions. For example, the plaza space was designed as a multi-functional area — reflecting pool, ice skating rink, performance plaza. This flexibility means that this space can be used in all seasons and is versatile enough to provide the citizens of Calgary with a multitude of entertainment experiences. On the other hand, this space is also viable as a passive, park-like environment.

Using a directional terracing motif, the space is arranged to provide an amphitheater setting, with all seating focused on the central plaza/skating rink/reflecting pool space. It is a dynamic area for a performance. A small, circular amphitheater at one corner of the square plaza provides a smaller, more intimate performance space. The precast concrete

ceremonial arcade, reminiscent in design of an Aztec temple, is sited to be viewed diagonally across the plaza as one enters the space. It's evident, in fact, that each aspect of the site has been carefully studied to concentrate the attention on the central activities, while at the same time, allowing small, intimate areas of rest and relaxation. One is aware at all times of the grandeur of the space and light, and yet the small, carefully controlled textures.

This balance of space, mass, color, texture and static and moving forms and surfaces creates an environment that is always in flux. The water cascading over stepped surfaces, the terraced lawn areas and the carefully articulated battered walls interspersed with plants all are testimony to a space designed for use and visual delight. Situated as it is, adjacent to the Municipal Buildings and the Calgary Center for the Performing Arts, this space is a focal point of the city. The citizens of Calgary are fortunate to have a space in which to spend their leisure time that not only served the needs of the 1988 Olympics, but also continues to serve as their activity hub both day and night.

Project
Olympic Plaza
Location
Calgary, Alberta, Canada
Design Firm
M. Paul Friedberg
Photographer
Ron Green

An Earth Sculpture Amphitheater

Using graded and sculpted earth as the primary building tool, the designers of *Hargreaves Associates* created an amphitheater in a multi-phased mixed-use project in suburban Denver. This space, *FIDDLER'S GREEN AMPHITHEATER,* planted simply with lawn and pine trees, developed from the designer's study of the ancient theatre of Dionysus. The 800-year evolution of the amphitheater was a concept that intrigued the designers.

In *FIDDLER'S GREEN,* an evolutionary process was also part of the design program. The designers were responsible for the initial grading and planting, but the owners would, eventually, install "a municipal overlay" on the earth forms — chain-link fencing, lighting, and additional planting. The designers state, "it remains to be seen if the basic power and simplicity of Phase I at Fiddler's Green can reassert itself as the facility becomes permanent." Judging from the initial installation, it would be extremely difficult to alter or mask the grandeur of these land forms. The graceful sweep of the curved sloping sides of the bowl and the care with which the designers laid out the site lines are not elements that can be easily disguised or altered with fencing or even planting.

At the present time, this space is not only used by the Denver Symphony as its summer home, it's also used by the occupants of the adjacent office workers as a place to have lunch and enjoy mini concerts and impromptu events. Eventually, when the planned regional

museum of art is built, the space will also incorporate an outdoor sculpture exhibition.

This space not only contributes to the use of leisure time in that it creates a place for entertainment, it also gives a focus to what could be a rather bleak landscape of suburban office sprawl. At the present moment it is, indeed, a marketing feature for Greenwood Plaza South. Beyond use of leisure time, however, the designers have used time in an entirely different way. The seasons, the cycles of nature and the inevitable passage of time are illustrated in this design that uses the earth and the elements of nature as the essence of decorative elements.

Project
Fiddler's Green
Location
Englewood, Colorado, USA
Client
John Madden Company
Design Firm
Hargreaves Associates: George Hargreaves,
principal
Awards
1984 Honor Award, ASLA
Photographer
Hargreaves Associates

In Opposition to
Geometry

The designers of *Joe Karr & Associates* used a series of pure circular forms to landscape the interior courtyard of the L-shaped *TERMAN ENGINEERING CENTER* on the Stanford University campus. The challenges of this site were not simple — two of the building's seven stories are situated below grade. How to bring light into these below-grade-level rooms was a problem to be solved. The solution creates a delightful play of movement and space that would not have been attempted without this building configuration. The voluptuous curving forms of the design are in contrast to the rectilinear geometry of the building form and the fenestration of the facade. The sinuous ramp-tie wall system that winds around four existing mature specimen trees (two silk oaks and two cedars) rises fourteen feet from a shallow (18-inch)

reflecting pool to the main site grade. The surface of this pool is at eye level when viewed from the rooms at the lowest level.

At the top of the ramp, a small semi-circular pool empties into a series of four circular basins that form a waterfall. This pure circular motif is carried further in the circular planters within the pool itself. The bottom of this shallow pool has been painted dark to give the illusion of depth. However, many students have been known to wade across to sit on the concrete curbs of the planters and the pool edge.

Around the two outside facades of the building, the designers further sculpted the land at a 45-degree angle to create light wells for the interior underground areas. At the base of these slopes, a concrete drainage tunnel serves a dual purpose by also acting as a seat height bench. Bridges over the light well serve as pedestrian walks to the entrances.

Overall, the sheer walls and sloped, terraced surfaces of this plan add not only interest, charm and usability to this site, they also provide that necessary ingredient

to human health — light. One also is
aware of the sense of play that this radical
sculpting has created — the sense that
one can travel up or down to different
areas where one can engage in leisure
time activities in a few short minutes. The
different experiences and different areas,
however, are still unified, still all of a
piece — something one feels in any
successful design solution.

Project
Terman Engineering Center, Stanford University
Location
Stanford University, Palo Alto, California, USA
Client
Stanford University
Landscape Architect
Joe Karr & Associates
Landscape Contractor
Economy Garden Supply Company
Architect
Harry Weese & Associates
General Contractor
F.W. Lathrop Construction Company
Photographer
Joe Karr & Associates

CHAPTER III

Public Spaces

At One with the City

More important to Washington than 'trust-busting' programs and national conservation legislation was the outcome of a conference of American architects held in the city in 1900, on the occasion of her first centennial. A commission appointed to prepare recommendations for an improved park system submitted a report in 1902 which called for sweeping changes in the layout of the whole city. Three members of the special commission had shared in planning the grounds and buildings for Chicago's Columbian Exposition. Daniel Burnham, its director, Frederick Olmstead, the noted landscape architect, and Augustus St. Gaudens, the most widely recognized of American sculptors, had learned from experience what enthusiasm and concerted effort could accomplish.

American Cities in the Growth of the Nation
Constance McLaughlin Green; Harper & Row, New York, 1965

The New College Edition The American Heritage DICTIONARY of the English Language defines *public* as:

1. Of, concerning, or affecting the community or the people: *the public good.* 2. Maintained for used by the people or community: *a public park ...*

In this chapter both definitions apply. The designs on the following pages deal with those spaces that affect the people and the community as a whole and contribute to the *public good.* Also, a great many of the spaces are public gardens, squares and parks, and the majority of these spaces are maintained by the community or other governmental agencies. However, there is another vital ingredient that all of these examples incorporate: the element of leisure time.

Vest-Pocket Parks, Parks & Playgrounds, Public Gardens, Exposition & Amusement Parks, Plazas & Urban Squares, Multi-Use Gardens — all these spaces are places where we spend whatever leisure time we have. Maybe it's only twenty minutes out of a lunch hour watching a waterfall, or an hour a weekend going to an amusement pier. Whatever the length of time, this period is set aside for refreshing the spirit, enjoying space, sunshine, plants and various activities meant to amuse and stimulate. This is a time set aside for play.

In sociological and historical terms, leisure time is a fairly recent phenomenon. Perhaps not until the nineteenth century and automation did the average person have the time to spend in enjoyment — other than the time set aside for religious holidays and other societally structured events. In terms of society and tradition, these events were carefully prescribed in terms of time and activities. Not so after the Industrial Revolution. Not so today. However, society still exerts some pressures in determining which forms of leisure activity and play are acceptable.

Play might be defined and categorized in many different ways. In fact, the definitions are so numerous it's very difficult to pick just one definition. For example, one might define it as recreation, relaxation or exercise, all of which are beneficial to the human body and spirit. Certainly studies have shown that human beings need a certain amount of exercise and relaxation to be "well-balanced" and "well." Scientific studies have also shown that children need to play, and need *spaces* to play in, in order to develop both physically and mentally. And where do they play in most urban environments? There is very little space for private gardens and backyards in most urban environments. So, the burden falls on the public sector to provide open green spaces for play, relaxation and recreation.

But let's examine that word, *burden.* If one stops to consider which cities of the world one considers the most desirable, the most beautiful, usually the ones that come to mind — e.g., Paris, Vienna, Constantinople, Venice, San Francisco, Leningrad — are cities with beneficent sites and/or multiple open areas of gardens, plazas, bodies of water and the like. These cities invite recreation and relaxation by the way in which they are sited and the ways in which the designers have provided usable public spaces. Usable, of course, meaning usable in one's leisure time.

THE CONCEPT OF LEISURE

The concept of leisure incorporates freedom and a release from time-consuming activities and responsibilities. Leisure time is for play, fun, idleness, contemplation — for whatever one chooses, and, to some extent, wherever one chooses. Combine, if you will, the idea that someone has the time, the *leisure* time to do whatever one chooses, wherever one chooses (within the limits of travel time from one site to another, of course) and you begin to develop a sense of the variety of Public Spaces a city or town can, and maybe even should, provide.

Incorporated into variety, of course, is the need to provide activities for all segments of the population. Here is where the landscape designer/urban planner must have studies of the age range of the population. Scale, level and complexity of activities are important considerations when you set about creating Public Spaces for the leisure activities of a whole population. What a child needs in terms of play space may be entirely different from what a senior citizen needs in terms of recreation space. There is also the concept of creating spaces for the interaction of divergent groups within the population — do you separate or integrate?

HOMOGENEOUS VERSUS HETEROGENEOUS

There are many schools of thought on the structure and components of Public Spaces. Function, of course, is of primary importance in terms of providing spaces for specific games and activities that occur in the public, rather than the private sector. There are also safety considerations in public spaces. How do you provide spaces for play and relaxation that provide the minimum risk for the user? How do you determine what to put where?

This book does not attempt to provide answers to any of these questions. Instead, by showing examples of how different designers

have solved these complex problems, this book is attempting to contribute to the wealth of solutions, and, indeed, to stimulate new ones. If one attempts to give one answer as the final and/or best solution, one, in essence, negates the focus of landscape design — design as an evolving entity. To further expand on this idea let's briefly explore the various aspects of Public Space — Vest-Pocket Parks, Parks & Playgrounds, Public Gardens, Exposition & Amusement Parks, Plazas & Urban Squares, Multi-Use Gardens — in terms of how each of these specific design forms fills a need in our contemporary society.

DIFFERENT FORMS FOR DIFFERENT FUNCTIONS

The Vest-Pocket Park is perhaps one of the most contemporary solutions to the problem of recreational space in the "urban-scape." Using one small lot to create either a space to play or a space to relax fulfills a definitive need in today's over-crowded cities. One must always keep in mind, however, the high cost of these installations. Not just the cost of the design, materials and installation, but the cost of the land and the potential return on the developed land. Here one must think not in terms of monetary return on the investment, but in terms of improvement of health and lifestyle.

Parks & Playgrounds contribute to the physical and psychological health of city dwellers. They are also necessary to the inhabitants of small cities and towns. Organized spaces for play and games can unite communities and build bonds between both individuals and neighborhoods. They can provide a focus where individuals come together in a common purpose.

Public Gardens, Exposition & Amusement Parks also provide a focus for individuals to come together, but the common purpose might not be quite so common. Whereas in Parks & Playgrounds the areas are designed for common and communal games and activities, the Public Gardens, Exposition & Amusement Parks provide a communal place for more individual

activities. People might come together, but there are diverse activities for individual enjoyment. The same might also be said for those areas we've categorized as Multi-Use Gardens. In some cases, Multi-Use Gardens might incorporate all the aspects of Public Spaces in one area — even community activities.

ON BEING A CITIZEN

Community activities, which are both enjoyable and beneficial to the community, are yet another aspect of how we spend our free time. And the place where many of these activities take place — Plazas & Urban Squares — are perhaps the category that has the most historical precedent.

One might say that the space in front of the cathedral in the Middle Ages was the beginning of the town square, the urban plaza. Certainly strolling musicians held sway from time to time, and passion plays where put on with the blessing of the church. If one wants to go back farther into history, consider the Greek agora. In his book, "*How the Greeks Built Cities*," R.E. Wycherley states:

> The agora was in fact no mere public place but the central zone of the city, its living heart ... It was the constant resort of all citizens, and it did not spring to life on special occasions, but was the daily scene of social life, business and politics.

One might venture to say that in all societies, both Eastern and Western, throughout the ages, Plazas & Urban Squares as a design from have either grown up or been designed and implemented. People need places to congregate, exchange gossip, sell wares and even conduct governmental or private business. These public spaces, then, are an essential part of everyday living.

All of the public spaces illustrated on the next pages are a part of everyday living and will become more so. Leisure time is an essential part of our daily lives. The predictions are that in the future we will have more, not less leisure time. How and where we spend this time is a vital component of our environmental tapestry.

In the Heart of Midtown

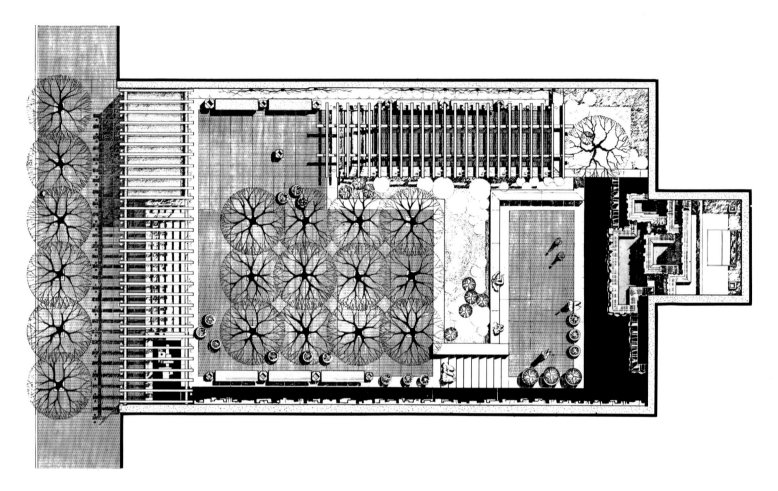

Sight. Sound. Smell. Touch. All these senses were appealed to in the design of *GREENACRE PARK* in midtown Manhattan. When conceptualizing and organizing this space, the designers of *Sasaki Associates* understood that the executed design had to be an environment in contrast to the pushing throngs and tension of everyday life in one of the world's largest, noisiest and busiest cities.

The client (The Greenacre Foundation) had a goal: to provide "a place where the general public can gain special repose from the increasing city experience of noise and concrete." The designers' task, of course, was to translate this goal, this concept, this dream, into an actuality on a site the size of a tennis court. An additional problem was that the site was

surrounded by tall buildings. The site definitely was not attractive nor desirable in terms of indigenous attributes. The designers, however, were undaunted.

To create the sense of space, they organized this public park space into three separate areas on three separate levels. The visitor, on entering, has a choice. The central area, which one enters, is a brick-paved sitting area shaded by honey locust trees. Under this canopy, one can sit at the movable tables and chairs and eat lunch, read, or chat with friends or

strangers. If this isn't immediately appealing, there is the raised terrace area along one side of the park, where there are also movable tables and chairs, and space for similar activities. There is, however, one major difference that distinguishes the two areas. The raised terrace is protected by more than a canopy of trees. The designers have added a transparent acrylic trellis roof that protects the visitors from the elements, but also allows light to enter this small space. In addition, the trellis is equipped with radiant heat for cold weather. The park, then, is not just a space for use in good weather. At any

time of the year, one can find peace and solitude here, perhaps at the third level, at the rear, more than in the two sitting areas.

This rear level is the lowest level. The designers have created a twenty-five-foot-high sculpted granite wall as a way to provide a waterfall. The sight of the cascading water provides a visual focus for the park and the sound masks the city sounds of traffic, horns, sirens and confusion. Enclosed by vine-covered walls, the whole area, with its flowering shrubs and pots of seasonal flowers, cuts down on the city sounds.

The water, rocks and plants in carefully thought-out geometric configurations give space and scale to a small site that, in large measure, gives solace and peace of mind to those inhabitants of the city that long for a place to reestablish contract with the natural wood. The popularity of this space (at least 10,000 visitors per week) attests to the fact that more spaces of this kind should be considered for every major urban area.

Project
Greenacre Park
Location
New York, New York, USA
Client
The Greenacre Foundation
Design Firm
Sasaki Associates, Inc.
Plans and Drawings
Sasaki Associates, Inc.
Photographer
© Felice Frankel

A Space for Tranquil Viewing

The *COOK ASSOCIATES COURTYARD* in Chicago, Illinois, is designed to be viewed both from ground level and from the upper stories of the adjoining office building. In organizing this semi-public space, the designers of *Joe Karr & Associates* used simple geometric configurations and low maintenance plantings to create a small "vest-pocket" garden that could be used for simply sitting in a peaceful setting, holding small meetings, informal gatherings, and even art exhibits.

The lushness of this four-season garden has been achieved by using a variety of plantings of different scale and texture.

The shape and color of one plant material is contrasted with another. Care seems to have been taken in selecting just the right leaf shape to contrast with another adjacent leaf shape. One has the sense of the careful study and arrangement that exist in Japanese rock gardens. The height of each type of planting also appears to

be thought out, and this adds to the sense of verdant green, although the space is narrow and constrained.

One almost has the feeling that this could have been a prosaic, utilitarian public space (perhaps just an extension of the sidewalk into the building entrances) but for the imagination and skill of the designer. The entrance into the courtyard, with the beautifully scaled and executed fence and gate, provides a barrier from the street, but at the same time, allows passers-by the opportunity to view the garden from the street. The openness of the fence design also brings light and space into the garden in a way that visually enclosing the space would not have done.

Paving patterns also provide a sense of space and visual directional elements.

Each entrance, for example, is articulated by a paved court, while planting areas are used to separate and define the areas. Heavier plantings are used in the interior spaces against the massive, high brick walls, breaking up the monotony of the vertical areas, while light, semi-transparent plantings are used against the exterior fencing. Flowering shrubs provide color accents, and the espaliered vines promise an ever-growing and changing lushness to the area. The eye will always be delighted, no matter what the season.

From whatever vista this space is viewed — above, inside, through the fence or from across the street — the view will continue to charm and proclaim the ability of man to integrate the best of the natural environment within the limitations of the urban, built environment.

Project
Cook Associates Courtyard
Location
Chicago, Illinois, USA
Design Firm
Joe Karr & Associates
Photographer
Joe Karr & Associates

A Pueblo Renaissance

"**U**nquestionably *public* in nature and design, the goal of the project was to reassert a public open space as the principal downtown focal image for San Jose." This statement from *Hargreaves Associates* describes both the conceptual intent and the final execution of the design (or perhaps re-design) of *PLAZA PARK* in San Jose, California. The concept of public open space was, of course, vital to this 3.5-acre park, in that this site has served that function since the city's beginning as a pueblo in the eighteenth century.

Integrating the historical aspects of this era of the city's history into the design of the new park space was a challenge to the designers. Their response was to retain as much of the old as practical, while at the same time adding dynamic, contemporary elements in keeping with the growth and expansion of the city. For example, the wonderful, tall, existing mature trees were kept, along with the historic route of Old Monterey Road, the Camino Real that ran from southern to northern California, linking the Franciscan Missions. In fact, the designers used this route as the central promenade, the axial spine, that runs the length of the park. In this way, they "layered" the new elements of design over existing historical elements. Even the new technologically exciting fountain is a "layered" expression. The fountain is built on the site of the old Victorian City Hall.

Sited at an asymmetrical angle to the side of the central spine, the programmed play of the mist and the water have been conceived to tell the story of San Jose's climate, geology and culture. The idea of this phased element came from the artesian wells that were discovered in the 1800s. These wells, of course, were a determining factor in the agricultural

evolution of the area. Another grid that mimics the fountain (jacaranda trees) is intended to recall the almond and prune orchards that gave way to the city expansion.

The phasing of the fountain supposedly mimics the water cycle through the course of the twenty-four-hour day. The fine mist of the morning represents the fog that comes into the valley from the Pacific Ocean. As the sun burns off the fog, the mist evolves into a bubbling spray. The spray becomes a grid of jets as the day wears on and the sun becomes higher. These jets start low and then build to regal plumes that seem as elegant as a chorus of precision dancers.

At night, the glass block of the fountain floor is lit from below and glows a luminous green reminiscent of computers and technology. The columns of water seem to be starships lifting off for the heavens. Both day and night the fountain evokes the past, present and future. The present, of course, includes the active use of the fountain by the public. Since the installation is at the same level as the grade of the surrounding walks, access to the water is unrestricted, and the area has almost become a "swimming hole" for local inhabitants.

It is not only the public access and acceptance of this site that make it a success — the area is filled with people

day and night and used as a performance and ceremonial area — but the narrative of past and future give it a timeless ambiance. Perhaps this site can even become a living "time capsule," recording the evolution of this historic crossroads as the area continues to expand, grow and contribute to the technology of the future.

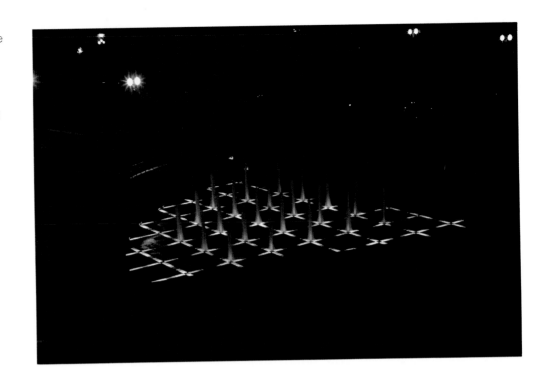

Project
Plaza Park
Location
San Jose, California, USA
Client
San Jose Redevelopment Agency
Design Firm
Hargreaves Associates: George Hargreaves, principal
Photographer
Hargreaves Associates
Awards
1989 Outstanding Public Landscape Design, California Garden Club; 1989 Special Efforts Award, California Landscape Contractor's Association

Esthetics as a Reality

When presenting the 1988 annual Art Commission Awards for Excellence in Design, Edward A. Ames, president of the Art Commission of the City of New York, made this statement: "Esthetics is not a lofty or insular concept, but a reality that plays a tremendous role in humanizing our urban environment. A seemingly simple detail like a fence along a sidewalk or park can be either an appealing addition to the landscape or a rigid institutional barrier. The difference lies in the design..." Mr. Ames could have been speaking specifically of *Signe Nielsen's* design for *THE RECONSTRUCTION OF THREE PROSPECT EXPRESSWAY PARKS*. The thoughtful use of elegant details obviously was one of the reasons her design won an award in 1988.

The three parks — *TERRACE PARK, SEELEY PARK, VANDERBILT PARK* — that border the Prospect Expressway in Brooklyn create a charming promenade lined with trees. The segmented arc created by the three sites parallels the expressway. Ms. Nielsen used similar paving patterns and materials in all designs to unify the three sites as parts of

a whole, and managed (with some difficulties) to create play areas, verdant lush plantings, plaza spaces and quiet sitting areas within the project.

The difficulties Ms. Nielsen encountered were primarily the community's concerns about the use of the parks. Vanderbilt Park, for example, had been used as a "hang-out" and the community wanted it de-mapped. The community members were convinced, however, that through design this park could become a viable space. The newly-designed space has been opened up, and a central plaza for sitting organized with a gracious walkway at the rear of the site.

Another community concern was safety. For this reason (threats of liability), many aspects of the design were altered. The resulting schemes stress simplicity of form, space and materials, while at the same time offering a variety of activities for the neighborhood inhabitants.

The materials chosen for the reconstruction are, in many ways, similar to the indigenous materials of the parks — concrete, granite block borders and steel picket fencing. In fact, many of the existing materials were saved and refurbished. New concrete installations were designed to match existing scoring patterns, and color and existing trees were maintained in the design concept. The designer took great care to preserve the best of the existing design, while adding and

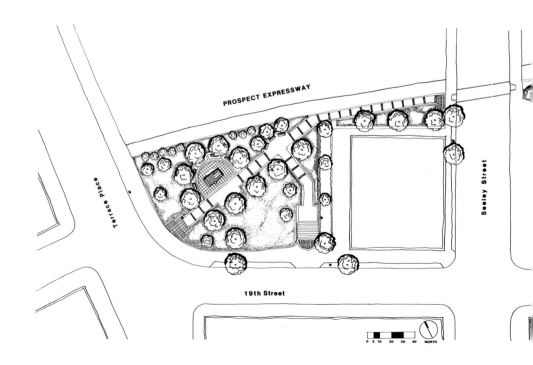

incorporating additional elements to facilitate use and safety.

Use and safety are, of course, essential elements of any viable public park installation in an urban area. No matter how attractive or esthetic a design concept is, if the public cannot use the space with comfort and a feeling of safety, then the design is not successful. In the case of the Reconstruction of Three Prospect Expressway Parks, Signe Nielsen, by working with the community, has created viable spaces for relaxation and recreation that enhance the neighborhood visually and help to restore the individual's spirit.

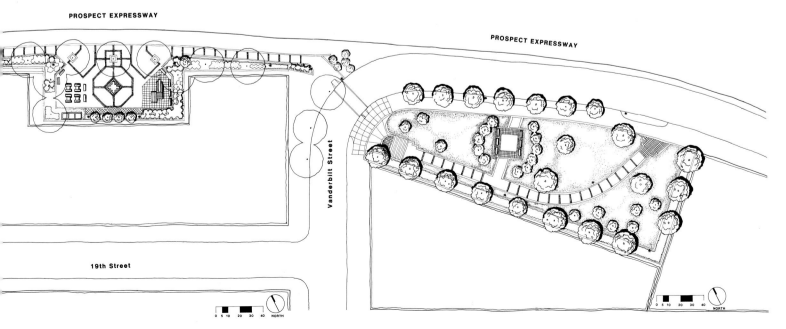

PROSPECT EXPRESSWAY

PROSPECT EXPRESSWAY

Vanderbilt Street

19th Street

0 5 10   20   30   40   NORTH

0 5 10   20   30   40   NORTH

Project
Prospect Expressway Parks: Terrace Park, Seeley
Park, Vanderbilt Park
Location
Brooklyn, New York, USA
Client
City of New York Parks and Recreation
Design Firm
Signe Nielsen Landscape Architect, PC: Signe
Nielsen, principal-in-charge; Mary Dalka Fouk,
Kim Mathews, project designers
Photographers
Signe Nielsen, James Morse
Awards
1987 Excellence in Design, Art Commission of
the City of New York

Using the Natural Environment of an Urban Center

When Frederick Law Olmsted designed Central Park in 1850, the concept of a children's playground was not part of the design vocabulary. When the Central Park Conservancy began to rehabilitate the park in recent years, however, the need for play space for children became apparent. As the result of a design competition, the office of M. *Paul Friedberg* was retained by the city to design one of the new major play spaces in the park at 67th Street, just off Fifth Avenue.

The resulting design — *67TH STREET PLAYGROUND* — has become a landmark in itself, nestled as it is in the rock outcropping of New York City's Central Park. Visible and accessible from Fifth Avenue, this carefully detailed space not only provides play space and activities for children of different ages and motor skills, it also provides areas for adults to sit, watch and relax. Special attention has also been given to accessibility for the handicapped in the wheelchair level and the handicapped play areas.

By using natural materials throughout (stones, logs, sand, water), the designers immediately integrated the design

elements into the existing natural topography of the park. The introduction of the 30-foot-long metal slide into rock outcropping not only enforces this cohesion of design and nature, it also promotes a play environment without perceived equipment. The natural environment dominates this site, and with the introduction of carefully designed elements of natural materials, provides "equipment" not only for play — swinging, exploring, climbing, etc. — but for social and cognitive experiences as well. The opportunities for creative play that such structures as the sway log, balance beam, tire platform/swing, suspension bridge and tree house provide perhaps can only be evaluated by the children themselves. all parts of the design are thought out in terms of how the children will perceive the space and how the adults can supervise without interfering. The sense of scale is a compelling factor in this design.

If one were to try to become child-size and enter into the mind of the child at play, it might be possible to sense the world created by the designers of M. Paul Friedberg's office. The island in the lake, accessible by both a stone bridge and a wooden bridge, could be a castle under siege surrounded by a moat. Stepping over, around and on the stepping columns

one might be a giant. The spring net and balance suspension bridge allow one to ford chasms and raging rivers. Such is the wonder of the child's mind challenged by neutral and integrated materials that allow free rein to the imagination.

Frederick Law Olmsted would not be unhappy with this addition to his original design. None of the natural elements of the park has been supplanted in the search for play space for children. Quite the opposite. By designing this area as almost a microcosm of nature, the designers have given the children an education in appreciating the whole of Central Park and the natural environment.

Project
67th Street Playground
Location
New York, New York, USA
Client
City of New York
Design Firm
M. Paul Friedberg
Photographer
Ron Green

Contemplation of Monuments

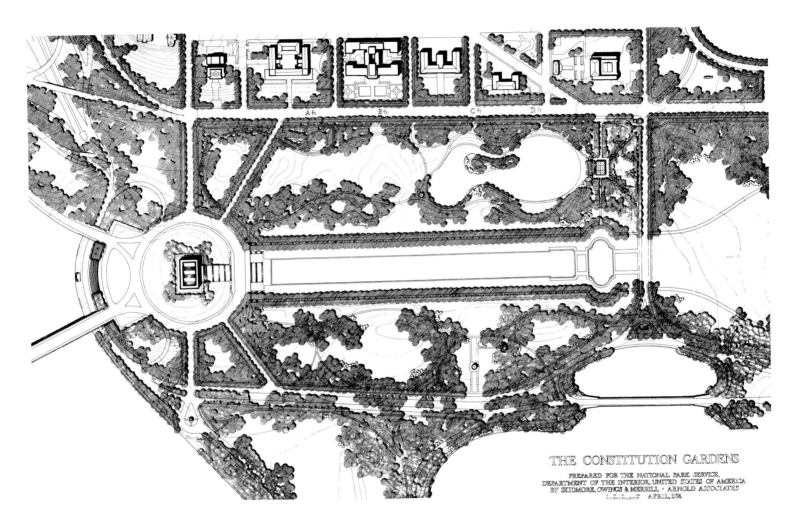

THE CONSTITUTION GARDENS

PREPARED FOR THE NATIONAL PARK SERVICE,
DEPARTMENT OF THE INTERIOR, UNITED STATES OF AMERICA
BY SKIDMORE, OWINGS & MERRILL · ARNOLD ASSOCIATES
APRIL, 1974

Using meandering paths and a lake to reflect our national monuments, *Skidmore Owings & Merrill* in collaboration with *Arnold Associates* has created an expansive outdoor environment that provides spaces for multiple activities — outdoor exhibits, informal sports, picnics, bicycling, strolling and passive recreation generally. The designers' concept for the future allows works of art to be discretely located within the park for the visitor to discover and appreciate.

The *CONSTITUTION GARDENS*, covers a 45-acre site that was the World War I temporary Navy Munitions Buildings. This site, located between Constitution Avenue and the Lincoln Memorial reflecting pool on the Washington Mall, was designed and built for the bicentennial celebration of 1976. To achieve a sense of informality that invites the visitors to wander along the water's edge and contemplate our nation's cultural and historical heritage, the designers used curving lines, and gently rolling planes in contrast to the rigid formality and geometric linearity of the

reflecting pool, the Washington Monument and the Lincoln Memorial. The undulating paths and contoured meadows combine with the bermed edge along Constitution Avenue to play against the axial symmetry of Pierre Charles L'Enfant's city design for the federal city. The contrasting geometry of the park provides a relaxing foreground to contemplate the larger historic setting.

The essence of the gardens — an alternating large open meadow and wooded park — enhances views of the architectural monuments. The monuments define the past and put history in perspective so that it can be understood and encompassed. This park is alive, evolving, growing and changing with the seasons and the time of day. To understand a garden, the plants and land forms that make up a garden, one must contemplate it in all lights and in all seasons.

One must understand the transience and yet permanence of growing things. When one understands the cycles of nature, one can truly experience and appreciate the garden. In this, the designers have succeeded. They have collaborated in designing and producing an outdoor space that expresses the magnificence of our natural heritage while providing a backdrop for our historical heritage.

Project
Constitution Gardens
Location
The Washington Mall, Washington, D.C., USA
Design Firm
Skidmore, Owings & Merrill
Consultant
Arnold Associates

Activities on the Avenue

PERSHING PARK in Washington, D.C., was created from what was originally a group of traffic islands on Pennsylvania Avenue. The designers of M. *Paul Friedberg* were challenged to transform this busy vehicular site (two blocks from the White House and across the street from the restored Willard Hotel) into a viable recreation space. The program called for an ice skating rink and water area, as well as outdoor dining facilities and a monument — a monument to General Blackjack Pershing. In these requirements, the program also implied that the site be insulated and isolated from the traffic — the first conceptual problem to be solved.

The solution to the noise and congestion problem — the insulation and isolation of the site — was to use earth to physically buffer the site from the surrounding streets. A berm was constructed on three sides of the site, and

planted with grass and honey locust. This berm creates a world of green, peace and tranquility in the midst of Washington, D.C.'s preeminent street.

One might say that the peace and tranquility are brought about not just by the isolation from noise and the luxurious planting, but by the sense both of space and privacy within the block-long site. Perhaps the division of the site into three separate areas — monument area, entry/dining area, amphitheater/ice skating/pool area — contributes to this feeling of many different experiences within one site. The scale of the architectural elements, in fact, contributes to a feeling of a large site within a forest space. The waterfall, of course, might be the foremost example of the scale of this project. It juts out of the stepped seating area surrounding the amphitheater/ice

skating/pool area, thrusting its granite clad presence into the forefront. In addition to breaking up the stepped expanse and providing intimate pockets on either side, this form of cascading water also provides a dynamic sense of movement — not only the movement of the water, but a sense that the form itself is moving into and across the water. The form creates a thrust and sense of direction.

The designers counteracted what might have been an overpowering thrust, however, by articulating the surrounding steps with pockets of planting. These plantings have grown into lush elements that are changed with the season and which provide intimacy and privacy along the massive stepped expanse. In any urban environment, elements and moments of privacy are most welcome.

Washington, D.C., the nation's capital, is of course, a public city by definition. Not only do the myriad government

workers need public spaces in which to relax, the international company of tourists and visitors need spaces in which to regroup and process the wealth of visual information presented on a tour of this city. This space allows that. The sculpted architectural forms contrasted with the ever-evolving soft, lush plantings provide a space separate from Washington, D.C., yet in its almost larger than life dynamic elements, ever a part of it.

Project
Pershing Park
Location
Washington, D.C., USA
Design Firm
M. Paul Friedberg
Photographer
Ron Green

A Waterfront Tourist Attraction

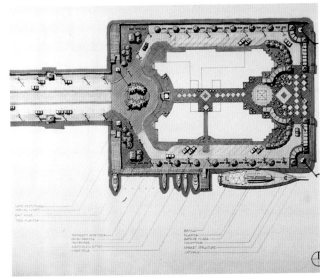

Project
St. Petersburg Municipal Pier
Location
St. Petersburg, Florida, USA
Design Firm
Sasaki & Associates, Inc.
Photographer
Tori Butt

Built in 1926 as a tourist attraction, the *ST. PETERSBURG MUNICIPAL PIER* languished through years of neglect. To revitalize this area, and promote public use and economic activity, the City of St. Petersburg retained *Sasaki Associates, Inc.* to revitalize both the pier and the visitors' building at the pierhead. The design resulting from this commission has promoted a record number of visitors, and the leasing of the space has exceeded projections. In effect, this project has become the catalyst for the city's continued revitalization of the waterfront.

The revitalization of the visitors' building — the pierhead — did not involve altering the structure or the exterior facade. The distinctive shape of the building was maintained, but a glass elevator was added to provide improved access as well as dramatic impact. Perhaps this improved access was in deference to the retirement aspects of St. Petersburg. The same might be said for the tramway that links the new land side parking area with the visitors' building.

St. Petersburg was one of the Florida cities to promote "residentism" — encouraging tourists to spend their retirement years in the city where they vacationed. Since this concept was promoted in the 1940s, the city's retirement population has grown. It makes sense, therefore, to design for the needs of a retirement population. Accessibility and transportation become important issues as people age. Entertainment and use of leisure time also become important issues, as does public space.

Addressing the issue of use of leisure time, the designers implemented the space in the visitors' building with an aquarium, food court, restaurant, community center, shops and an observation deck. Additional shop space was added on the pier in the colorfully roofed vendors' pavilions. People can stroll, chat, shop and interact. Horse-drawn carriages wend their way along the walkways, and colorful banners announce events and identify shops. Planting and paving add color and texture. Above all, a sense of color prevails over the pier, a sense of playfulness, a sense of responsibility and obligation suspended. A sense that the time has come at last to enjoy the simple things in life — the sea, the sun and time to enjoy human relationships.

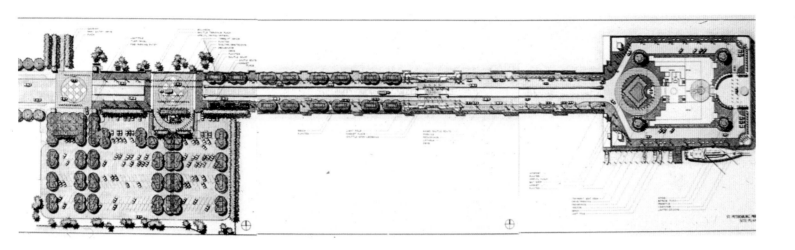

A Southern California Collaboration

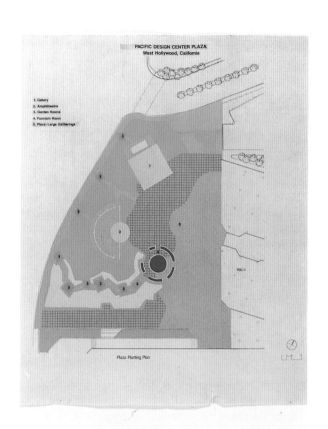

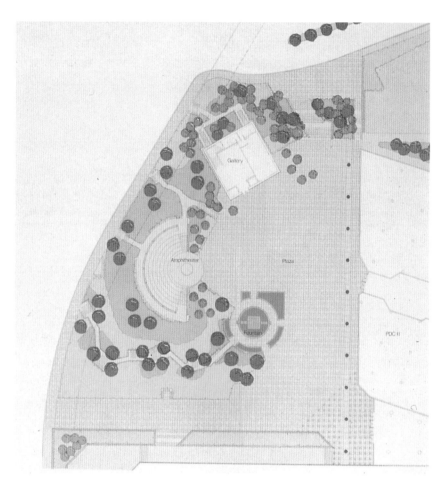

PACIFIC DESIGN CENTER PLAZA in West Hollywood, California, was designed to serve two purposes. The plaza was to be a space around which the Pacific Design Center (PDC) could expand, and it was also to serve as an open civic space, the plaza for the new city of West Hollywood. Given this two-part agenda, the designers of *Balmori Associates, Inc.* conceived a many faceted design that incorporated the agenda of both parties and, at the same time, created a space with an identity of its own.

Using highly articulated color and pattern in paving, and incorporating directional elements in walks and architectural elements, the resulting design provides both open public space and more intimate interactive space for the

visitor. One of the more intimate spaces is the main approach from San Vincente Boulevard (the new offices of West Hollywood are across San Vincente Boulevard). On this angled walk, small "garden rooms," designed to be used by small groups or individuals have been situated at the angles. This concept of "rooms" has been extended to the whole of the plaza itself.

At the end of the angled walk is the "water room." This "room" is created by a series of water jets and benches that provide the enclosure for a large fountain. Since this is the area that most people

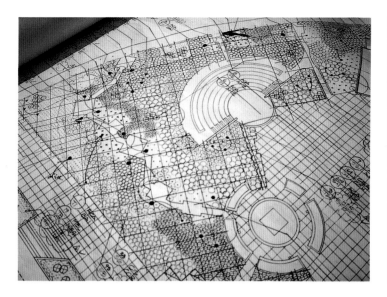

problems of Southern California have been taken into account by the designers, and none of the plants used needs constant watering. In this way, the sensitivity of the design solution allows the plaza to incorporate itself into the urban landscape and remain viable no matter what the environmental problems of the area.

Project
Pacific Design Center Plaza
Location
West Hollywood, California, USA
Client
Pacific Design Center
Design Firm
Cesar Pelli and Associates
Plaza Design
Diana Balmori
Design Team
Lily del Carmen Berrios, Alan Saucier, Peter Viteretto
Associate Landscape Architects
P.O.D., Los Angeles
Photographers
Joe C. Aker, Mark Lohman, Cesar Pelli and Associates, Joe Szasfai
Awards
1987 Progressive Architecture Award
1989 Merit Award, Connecticut Society of Architects

pass through, the "water room" and the fountain have been designed as the social area of the plaza. Another major area of the plaza is the 350-seat amphitheater. This is designed for large gatherings, as is the main area of the plaza.

This main plaza area abuts the free-standing gallery which will display the textiles and furniture designed in the PDC. The plaza will display festivals, fairs and other public gatherings. In essence it reminds one of the plazas in front of the cathedrals where the weekly markets and passion plays took place. In fact, there are echoes in this design of the California missions with their fountains, plazas and courtyards.

The plantings are another echo of California history. All the plant materials are dry-climate chaparral species indigenous to the area. The drought

Rooftops & Canyons

The paved, landscaped, rooftop development portion of *EMBARCADERO CENTER* in San Francisco is a narrow strip of land covering several blocks, situated between high-rise buildings. This area easily could have had the feel of a canyon were it not for the care taken to construct roof gardens, landscape the area and open it to large plaza across from the Ferry Building. Delightful and vibrant on sunny days, this area would also be charming on the cold, foggy, windy days that make up a large portion of San Francisco's weather forecast.

The designers of *John Portman & Associates* (assisted by *Sasaki, Dawson, DeMay Associates, Inc.*) were challenged by having to design a multi-block installation that would only be built one block at a time, and also by the selection of plant materials. The majority of the plants would have to survive on the roof gardens and also withstand the wind forces through this "canyon." For the majority of the planting, they chose ivy, flowering plants and trees that would

permit dappled light. The placement of the planting materials was another consideration. For the most part, the planting is concentrated around the structural elements and the edges of the plazas and walkways. Planting tubs are used for both trees and flowering plants and placed in and among tables, etc. Paving patterns are also important in this installation.

The paving of the areas within the "canyon" of Embarcadero Center are light-colored, appearing as a whole with the concrete structural members of the architecture, and in contrast to the plant materials. In the plaza across from the Ferry Building, brick pavers are used and the sculpture in the plaza is a light-colored concrete to tie the plaza back to the canyon. One has a sense of carefully thought-out details and color relationships to coordinate this project and visually bind the separate parts together.

Line and direction are important in creating a whole in this project. The horseshoe-shaped tunnel-like staircase that invites you to sample more than one level of the space, the vista of the Ferry Building tower that beckons you onward, the "crown" that rises gently through one of the rooftop structures — all these visual elements create interest and thus movement. The space would not be static even if there were no people striding or wandering through. This is perhaps what makes Embarcadero Center successful. There is the sense that through the next tunnel, at the top of the stairs, beyond the balcony lie more excitement, more magic.

Project
Embarcadero Center
Location
San Francisco, California, USA
Client
Embarcadero Center Ltd.
Design Firm
John Portman & Associates
Photographers
Michael Portman, Timothy Hursley
Consultants
Sasaki, Dawson, DeMay Associates, Inc.
Awards
1984 Urban Land Institute Award for Excellence

CHAPTER IV

Community & Urban Planning

The Scope of the City

Here is summarized the program of the planning of a city, in which it is exemplified that work is the human law and that there is enough of the ideal in the cult of beauty and order to endow life with splendor.

Tony Garnier: The Cite Industrielle
Dora Wiebenson; George Braziller, New York 1969

The planning and construction of a city on a specific un-populated site could be considered a fairly recent concept. In the past, cities grew up and evolved when a number of significant factors were present — drinking water supply, livable topography, suitable climate, natural resources, agricultural capacities, defense capabilities, trade routes, cultural likenesses and inheritance, cultural interaction and exchange of what one might call "universal ideas." If one studies the major cities of the world, it's obvious that the majority of these factors are present.

To take an arbitrary site and attempt to incorporate into a masterplan all these diverse factors can be a monumental task. But not an impossible one. It was done in 1956, for example, when the site for Brasilia was chosen by a commission. The 1963 Edition of the *Encyclopedia Britannica* states:

> No site for a city has been so carefully chosen. Consideration was given to topography, climate, drainage, water supply, geology, soils, land use, engineering power, transportation, recreation, building materials, public administration, scenery, and the general relation of man to his surroundings.

Oscar Niemeyer, a renowned and talented Brazilian architect, was commissioned to design the major governmental buildings on the city plan that Lucio Costa had designed in the shape of a huge cross which he described as the first gesture someone makes when they take possession of a place. It was an auspicious beginning, but it had in it the seeds of failure. Again, in landscape design, in urban and community planning, there is always the concept of time. And, in this case, it was the concept of evolutionary time.

THE EVOLUTION OF A CITY — The Process of Growth

The plan of Brasilia was a static form. It was elegantly conceived, but lacking the opportunity for spontaneous growth and evolution. A city is never static. In many ways cities are like living organisms. Sometimes they grow in one direction, sometimes in another. Sometimes they spread out horizontally and sometimes vertically. But there must be the opportunity to spread out and, when necessary, to reshape themselves to meet the needs of the time and the population.

In Brasilia, because there was no opportunity for growth, a series of satellite towns formed around the perimeter. It was a spontaneous phenomenon, but not one that the designers foresaw. It was a phenomenon that any designer of today, however, should build into the masterplan. How is this new town or new community or new area going to evolve? Where is the space for growth? Where are the factors — and sometimes these factors are, indeed, elusive and undefinable — that will allow this city, town or community to thrive and grow? These are not easy design tasks. But necessary tasks in both the conception and implementation of this aspect of landscape design.

THE FACETS OF COMMUNITY & URBAN PLANNING

To illustrate this concept of evolutionary time in the concept of Community & Urban Planning, we've divided this chapter into the following categories: Regional & Town Planning, Urban Redevelopment, Circulation Corridors, Waterways & Waterfronts, Environmental & Conservation Projects. Some of these categories may seem arbitrary, but for the most part they are an attempt to separate and discuss some of the complex issues facing the urban and regional planner with specific illustrations.

Regional & Town Planning is perhaps the most straightforward of the categories and includes primarily those projects where a new town or community has been designed on a previously unoccupied site, much like Brasilia. The economic base is always a vital issue in these projects. Who funds them? Who are the potential inhabitants? Some are funded by developers who see a market for housing and the related services. Others are funded by corporations who are, in effect, building a "company town." But, whoever funds them, the issue is, will they evolve, and thrive?

Urban Redevelopment, on the other hand, is concerned with a revitalization process in areas that have not continued to grow and prosper. For example, many "center cities," downtowns, have declined and gone into disrepair with the advent of the shopping center. Some of the projects illustrated will show downtowns that have once again become vital growth areas of a city. Here the concept of evolutionary time is illustrated by showing not just the process of disuse and decay, but the process of revitalization and, sometimes, new use for existing areas. Many of these projects seem to be the phoenix, the bird of Egyptian mythology, consuming itself by fire after 500 years and then rising renewed from the ashes.

HIGHWAYS, BYWAYS & WATERWAYS

Circulation Corridors is another area of landscape design that needs constant renewal. This category is defined as those areas between cities or areas of a city through which we travel or through which we organize our utilities — electricity, gas, telephone and so forth. These areas can either be wastelands, or attractive parts of the town and cityscape.

Street tree planting is part of this category. The use of landscape design to establish patterns of connection between buildings, streets and open spaces is another. How to treat Circulation Corridors is perhaps one of the most challenging aspects of

landscape design, and one that requires careful study in terms of the evolving aspects of the design.

When a designer is concentrating on an arborization plan, for example, it's not just the placement of the trees and other plant materials that's important. How soon and in what ways the trees and other plant materials will grow is vitally important. How long will the inhabitants have to wait for shade? What happens in different climates and different seasons? And, perhaps, most important — is the capacity for change built into the design? Can the city grow and evolve along with this arborization pattern, or is the design itself a static entity?

On the other hand, designs and patterns for Waterways & Waterfronts cannot be static since water is an ever-moving, ever-evolving entity and can change its course or the nature of the beach at will. Unless, of course, a waterway, i.e., a riverbed, is transformed into a concrete channel of sorts, and even then, rivers have been known to overflow their banks. It would seem, then, that along with the development and planting of a waterfront, one would have to plan for floods, tides, and other natural cycles and patterns of nature that one associates with waterways — conservation and environmental issues. In point of fact, the majority of categories of landscape design deal with elements of conservation and environmental issues, since landscape design cannot truly be separated from the environment.

CONTAINING & MAINTAINING THE NATURAL ENVIRONMENT

Environmental & Conservation Projects, this interdependent category, is concerned with those aspects of a landscape design project that seek to conserve and maintain both the natural and the man-made environment.

One of the examples shows how the necessity of using a retention pond on the site focused the design into new

and unique configurations of benefit, both to the environment and the users of the site. That would seem to be an eminently successful design solution — the environmental restrictions used in the interest of the design. From a sociological standpoint, of course, this seems to be one of the major issues of our time — maintaining and restoring the landscape for the benefit of man and for future generations. At the same time, however, there is the heritage of the past. How do we deal with that? What pieces of the past do we save for the citizens of the future? What Inspirational & Historic Spaces are worth restoring, maintaining — or creating?

Downtown in the Suburbs

"... a series of connected urban spaces going from formal to informal." This is the way *Alan Ward* of *Sasaki Associates, Inc.* describes the plan of *RESTON TOWN CENTER* in Reston, Virginia. Begun and developed with the idea that this would be "the complete suburb," it has become apparent that in the Reston of today there is no "downtown," no "heart," no focus to the suburb; residents have adopted a neighborhood plaza at a neighboring village as their "surrogate" downtown. To bring back a sense of community, Reston Town Associates was formed to create a downtown, a town center — Reston Town Center.

RTKL Associates of Baltimore did the masterplanning and the Phase I buildings, and *Sasaki Associates, Inc.* was commissioned to do the landscaping. It's interesting to note that the street layout of the town center is grid-like and urban in feeling and in opposition to the winding, curvilinear streets of the suburb. Alan Ward describes the decision this way: "A lot of the precedents that are being used now to organize new towns in the suburbs are urban models ..." At this point one has to question why the urban model is applied in the suburb.

Organization, focus and concentration might be the keys here. And perhaps a way to integrate nature with man-made structures. After all, many people move to the suburbs to incorporate at least some natural elements into their lives and habitation. Shopping and conducting business in a "downtown," however, poses different problems. Perhaps scale is the key.

If one lives in the suburbs one can go to the nearest city to conduct business and shop. That leaves the suburb a "bedroom" community. Obviously, the residents of Reston feel a loyalty to their town and want it to be a viable community: thus, the "downtown." In this plan, the 400-acre site of former woodlands has been organized into a grid pattern of buildings interspersed with open spaces. The four major open spaces have been designed as park spaces.

The first park space is Fountain Square, a paved, horseshoe-shaped area in the midst of trees and shops. The second park is reminiscent of a town square in New England with trees and criss-crossing paths. The third is an oval configuration set in a residential area, while the fourth is a "romantic" park complete with lake, islands and green belt. A transition from the "urban" features of the "downtown" to the natural, somewhat rustic features of the wooded suburb.

In this plan, the designers appear to have collaborated to provide a much needed center to this famous suburb. In a way, perhaps, they might be righting a wrong, providing something the original designs failed to foresee. One might look at it another way, however. All viable communities change, alter and grow if they are to survive. Perhaps Reston has grown into the need for a "downtown."

Reston Town Center
Location
Reston, Virginia, USA
Design Firm
Sasaki Associates, Inc.
Plans and Drawings
Sasaki Associates, Inc.
Photographer
Max MacKenzie

Environmental Integration

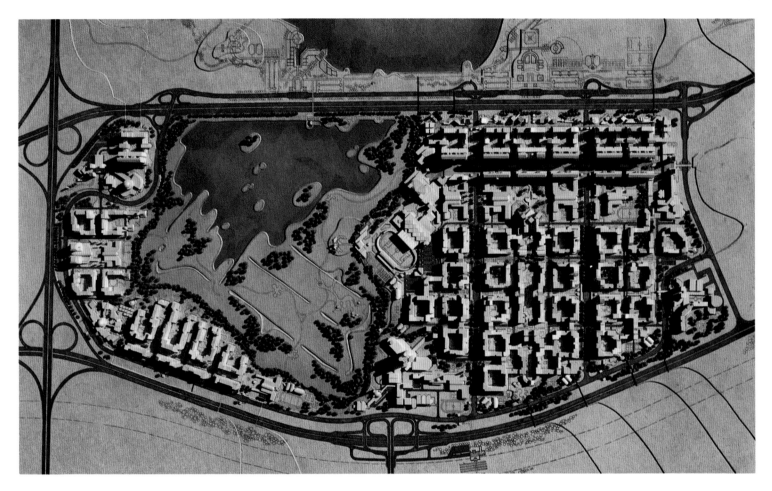

At the edge of the city of Minsk in the USSR, *Peter Gal* designed a complex of flats for 50,000 inhabitants — *DWELLING AREA "DROZDY."* The parameters for the design of this housing complex included the integration of the ecological protected zone, "Swansea," into this urban configuration. Or, perhaps one might say that the urban configuration was wrapped around the ecological zone.

In this "town plan," there is a sense of the formal, of traditional urban planning; the design is grid-like and rigid in the configuration of the structures of the flats. Yet, at the same time, there is freedom in the natural space with the wooded and wet areas — as though the designer held

the natural environment in such respect that he was loath to impose his ideas and restraints. Not so in the "biocorridors."

In the "biocorridors" (those formal open and recreation spaces crossing the blocks of flats) one feels the natural is held in restraint and made to conform to the tastes and needs of the human inhabitants. There seem, therefore, to be three levels to this design; the natural environment in its natural state; the natural environment as tamed by man and made useful for open

space and recreation; the man-made environment of the blocks of flats useful for shelter and protection against the elements.

In this the designer was sensitive to both the urban and the natural. The area is high-density; it sits at the edge of a major industrial city. To incorporate the natural to this extent not only preserves a large portion of the natural environment, it enhances the lives of the residents of this urban area.

Project
Dwelling Area "Drozdy"
Location
Minsk, USSR
Client
Minsky Gorodskoy Sowiet
Design Firm
Faculty of Architecture - Peter Gal, Juraj Furdik, Pavel Kosnac, Jane & Sergei Pastorok

A Downtown Success

Covering six and one-half city blocks, *HORTON PLAZA* has reclaimed a decayed area of downtown San Diego and turned it into a contemporary California version of a Medieval European village replete with commerce and habitation. This mixed-use, multi-level development is a product of a "visionary" architect, Jon Jerde. The Jerde Partnership specializes in retail space and revitalizing distressed and decayed commercial areas.

In downtown San Diego the raw material was an H-shaped, roofed shopping center. Jon Jerde removed the roof, twisted the straight line orientation and filled the space with nooks, balconies, bridges, arches, planters, lights and color. What he achieved is texture, interest and a desire to see what happens around the next corner, through the next arch, beyond the wall. The complex feels organically grown instead of designed on a drafting board. The eclectic mix of styles, in part, accounts for this.

The styles, when studied, seem taken from all aspects of California's legacy — historic, commercial, environmental. The Spanish Colonial reflects the city's historic past; the Moorish, perhaps, is reminiscent of the twenties and mansions of movie stars and movie palaces; the Victorian speaks of marvelous wooden houses from the turn of the century; and the contemporary, of course, is the heritage of the moment, today.

The mix of these styles may seem disparate, but the space between and the pastel colors used throughout are unifying themes. Street furniture, carefully placed, mature plantings and light are also used to create a whole from the parts. Topiary bushes (hippopotamuses and other animals) are used with other plantings to enforce the sense of charm and playfulness of the center. The paving patterns here, too, are an important ingredient in directional flow and texture.

Fine arts have also played a significant role in this complex. One million dollars have gone for such works as "The Obelisk"

Complementary Halves

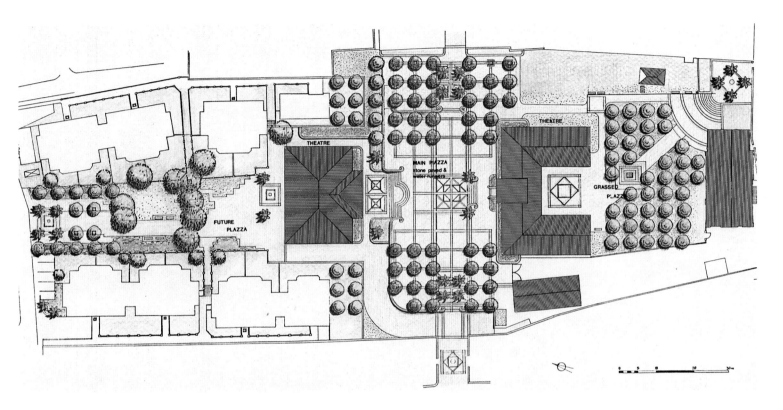

The *PIAZZA OF THE NEVE TZEDEK DANCE AND THEATER CENTER* was created near the Tel Aviv central business district in 1987. In what was once a Jewish neighborhood north of Jaffa (established in 1883), two abandoned school buildings (one for boys, one for girls) were renovated to establish a cultural center for theater and dance. In order to create a whole, a center, from these two separate structures a unifying motif had to be established.

The unifying motif was a piazza. The road that ran between the two buildings was closed off and the resulting space articulated with sandstone paving, steps and walls. Carefully placed trees were planted, some in articulated, simple planting boxes complete with water runnels paved in blue ceramic tiles. The sound of running water is a quiet counterpoint to the activity of the piazza.

In keeping with the classic simplicity of the two buildings, the details of the piazza are simple and elegant. The planting of the citrus groves and the mature date palms are statements both of the arid

environment of Israel and the formality of the site. Date palms in pairs or quartets stand at entrances to the buildings and the piazza. The citrus trees are planted in formal rows to eventually provide a green ceiling to areas of the space. The orientation of the site is also formal, running along a central axis through carefully thought-out stepped areas.

There are three stepped areas, three sub areas, in the major piazza space

between the buildings. The minimalist style in which this space is designed emphasizes the carefully proportioned details of the two structures and plays them against each other and the stark blue of the desert sky. At night the lighting system — uplighting of the buildings and citrus groves, surface lighting of the piazza with low recessed fixtures, nineteenth-century

design lighting fixtures — creates a dramatic scenario, emphasizing the design details of the location.

There is also a grassed piazza at the rear of one of the theater buildings. An additional citrus grove has been planted around an artesian well discovered at the rear of one of the theaters. This well was discovered during the excavation work and an immediate change was made in the design to incorporate this resource. Additional sitting steps of sandstone were

added to the well's retaining walls of local sandstone.

This adaptation and inclusion of the artesian well is much like the concept of the original renovation and adaptive reuse of these school buildings for a cultural center. All the old historic structures have been refurbished and reused in combination with new planting and paving of indigenous materials. The feeling of oasis is present in the shade of the trees and the gently running water. What could be more an expression of the heritage of the country?

Project
Piazza of the Neve Tzedek Dance and Theater Center
Location
Tel Aviv, Israel

Transportation in a Greenhouse

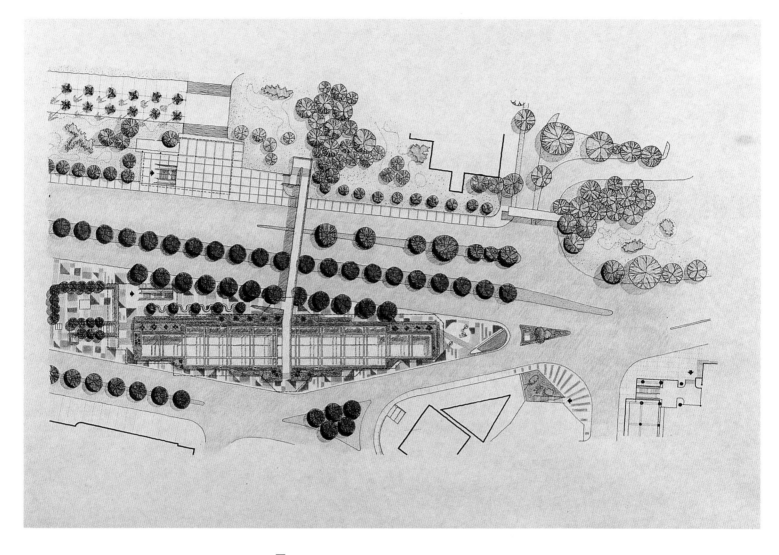

The *PARQUE DEL ESTE STATION* in Caracas, Venezuela, is, in effect, a combination of transportation hub and giant greenhouse. This station, constructed in a park designed by the Brazilian landscape architect, Burle Marx, has used the lush green foliage of the park and surrounding landscape as a design motif for the station. Plants are used throughout the structure, from the rafters to the floor.

By using this extensive planting combined with the translucent glass covering the giant space frame, one has the feeling that the barriers between the outside and the inside are fragile and amorphous. The planting at the south side of the station — *Hymenocallis caribaea, Acalypha wilkesiana, Philodendro bipinattifidum, Arecastrum romanzoffianum* — is low and hardy for the most part, with the palms used as accents under the roofed patio areas. A wide variety of palms were used in the project for texture and dramatic effect. Great care was taken with each species to make sure that the level of light was adequate. In the south part of the station plants that thrive in sun and shadow have been selected, but in the north part of the station all the plants selected are those that will do well in shade. Many of the plants have been installed to hang in the interior space, while others cascade down from the interior concrete structural forms, nothing seeming to be in opposition to the high-tech structure of the station.

This balanced installation, which successfully integrates the natural environment with the sophisticated structural solutions to enclosing space, was designed and implemented by architects and landscape architects of C.A. *Metro de Caracas* and *Consorcio Grid APM, C.A.* The successful collaboration is evident in this innovative structure which does not obliterate the charming garden area, but hovers over and takes the garden into itself.

Project
Parque Del Este Station
Location
Caracas, Venezuela
Design Firms
C.A. Metro de Caracas and Consorcio Grid
APM, C.A.
Concept and Preliminary Drawings
C.A. Metro de Caracas, División de Arquitectur
y Diseño Ambiental: Max Pedemonte, architec
principal-in-charge; Freddy Jordán, architect,
design
Architectural Project
Consorcio Grid APM, C.A. Gustavo Niño,
architect, principal-in-charge; Leopoldo Sapen
architect
Landscaping
C.A. Metro de Caracas, División de Arquitectur
y Diseño Ambiental: Pablo Torres, architect

Re-creating & Restoring History

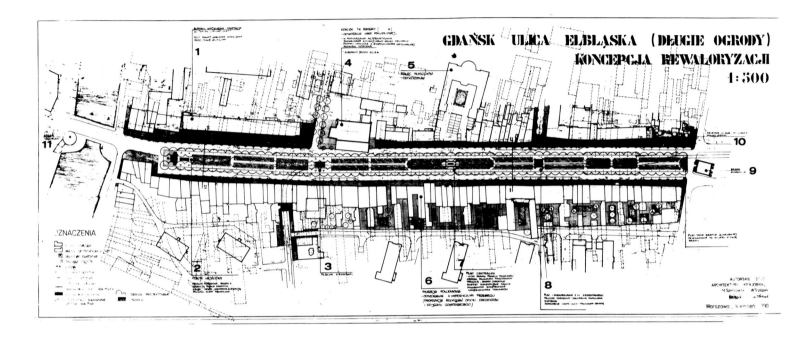

Landscape architects *Marek Szeniawski* and *Wojciech Trzopek*, of *asak Landscape Architecture Design Studio,* were asked to restore and re-establish the historical significance of *ELBLASKA STREET* (Long Gardens Street) in Gdansk, Poland. In order to accomplish this, the designers had certain criteria to meet.

The new frontages of the buildings had to be established, the old avenue with a speed limit of 30 kilometers per hour had to be restored, and a new proposal to restore the area around the remaining southern aisle of the Church of St. Barbara had to be developed. Taking these criteria into account, the architects developed a plan that included the old historic plantings and elements of the street — Vat Tower and Gate, and Zulawska Gate — while adding new plants and architectural elements that would unify the whole.

Using granite pavers, basalt pavers, paving stones and gravel, and incorporating the plantings such as *Tilia tomentosa, Tilia varsoviensis, Crataegus oxyacantha* "Paul's Scarlet," the designers created an Entrance Square with a garden pavilion, pool, sculpture and benches as well as a Church Square to define the plaza in front of St. Barbara Church. A Central Square was created opposite the Mniszech Palace, which like St. Barbara Church is to be restored.

Further along the street another Square with a cafe and garden pavilion has been established. The final Square is Zulawska Gate Square across from a new colonnade.

The street therefore begins with the Vat Gate and Tower — a legacy from Medieval times — and ends at the seventeenth-century Zulawska Gate paired with a late twentieth-century design. The history of Gdansk is told through the series of gates, towers and squares along a boulevard.

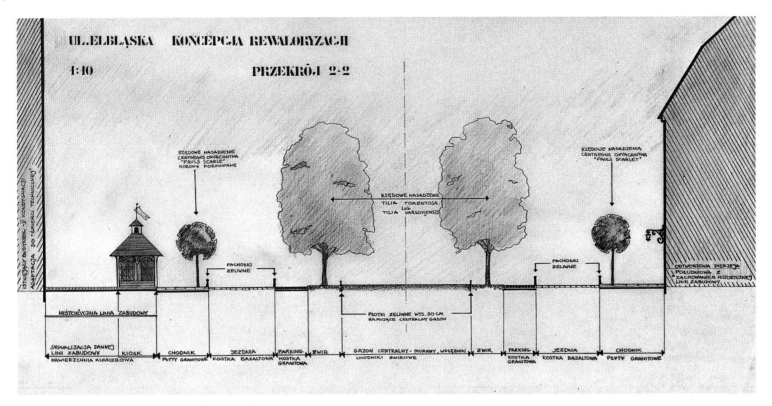

UL. ELBLĄSKA   KONCEPCJA REWALORYZACJI

1:10   PRZEKRÓJ 2-2

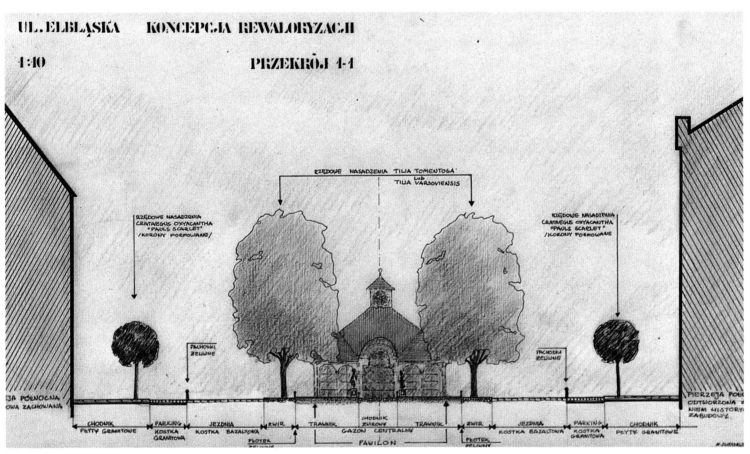

UL. ELBLĄSKA   KONCEPCJA REWALORYZACJI

1:10   PRZEKRÓJ 4-4

Project
Elblaska Street (Long Gardens Street)
Location
Gdansk, Poland
Client
Gdansk Centre for Documentation of Historical
Monuments
Design Firm
asak Landscape Architecture Design Studio:
Marek Szeniawski, Wojciech Trzopek, landscape
architects
Photographer
asak Landscape Architecture Design Studio
Consultant
Artur Kostarczyk, D.Sc. Architect

157

Ecological
Reconstruction

Roberto *Elvir Zelaya* has found that practicing landscape architecture in the public sector is more rewarding than practicing in the private sector — especially in the area of urban problems such as the destruction of natural resources, deforestation, ecological imbalance and endangered flora species. As the Planning Director of the Municipality of San Pedro Sula in Honduras, Central America, *Elvir Zelaya* has been responsible for instituting and implementing a 10-year program to accomplish the *ARBORIZATION OF SAN PEDRO SULA.*

In accomplishing an "arborization," the creation of arrangements of trees, one must first have trees. Since deforestation was a problem in this area, trees had to

be grown. To this end, the Municipal Nursery was revived and seed gemination of the desired species was begun. Approximately 50 indigenous species were selected for the replanting program.

This program took in extensive areas of the boulevard that circles the city and transformed them into green belts with trees and pedestrian walks. Flowering trees — *Cassia fistula* and *Tabebuia rosea* — native to the area, adapted to the environment, were used widely to provide color, texture, shade and directional elements. Hundreds of San Juan trees *(Tabebuia donnel)* have been planted along with western section of the boulevard. These trees with their yellow flowers, in effect, ring the city. In addition, Macuelizo *(Tabebuia rosea)* has been planted along Boulevard Morazan, a

street almost devoid of trees. These flowering trees will create a "roof" of pink along the thoroughfare.

African palms, however, were not originally native to the area, but are very prevalent in Honduras because of industrial use of African palm nuts. *Vetchias* and *pink Tabebuias* have been transplanted in among the African palms to expand and reinforce the landscaping around the few remaining trees on the boulevard. Perhaps one of the positive aspects of this project is that the designer was concerned not only with just propagating native species, but also with utilizing the existing natural elements of the site — the rocks, for example.

Since the geology of the site provides an abundance of rocks, they have been used to create rock gardens, paving and

focal points. Rock gardens have been planted with such species as *Gardenia* vines, *Seagrus* palms, *Delonix reggia* and *Cannas,* and these small areas install a sense of scale and intimacy in the rows of street trees which are the predominant force of this plan. The mountain range that abuts the city installs a different sense of scale — one of majesty and grandeur.

Merendon Mountains (among the highest peaks in Central America) have been a protected reserve since the area was damaged extensively by hurricane Fifi in 1974. Since San Pedro Sula depends on this mountain range for its water supply, perhaps that disaster helped to provoke the inhabitants into reexamining their commitment to what could be a tenuous environment.

To further enhance this project, small parks and public spaces have been refurbished, modified and created along the city's principal streets. Some serve as memorials to the heroes of Central America and to events that have altered the history of San Pedro Sula. Certainly, this project will alter the history of San Pedro Sula and perhaps even the whole of Central America. Already the number of established trees has exceeded 150,000, a conservation area of native flora on a 240-hectare park is planned and the area has become a "school" for programs in other Honduran cities. The project has also captured the attention of other Third World cities with similar problems of deforestation, etc. Perhaps "arborization" could become a universal concept.

Project
Arborization of the City of San Pedro Sula
Location
San Pedro Sula, Honduras, Central America
Client
Municipalidad de San Pedro Sula
Design Firm
Municipalidad de San Pedro Sula: Roberto Elvir Zelaya, landscape architect; Jeronimo Sandoval S., mayor
Photographer
Roberto Elvir Zelaya

Transforming an Industrial Junkyard

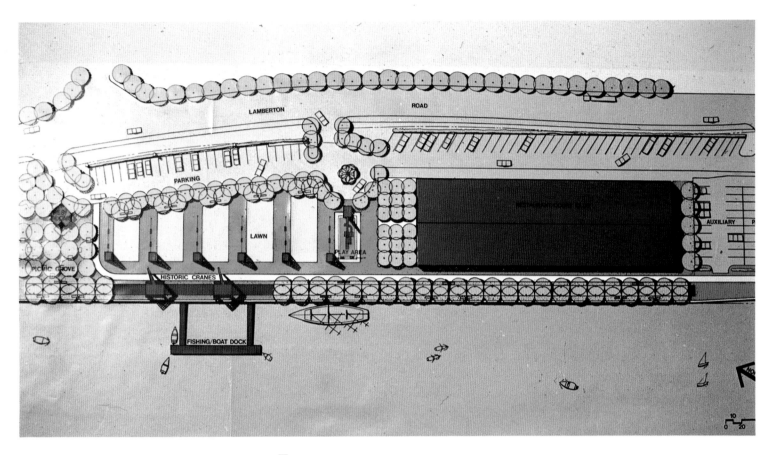

TRENTON MARINE TERMINAL PARK is a result of the foresight of the New Jersey Economic Development Authority and the creativity of *Arnold Associates*, Landscape Architects. This 2.5-acre park is located on the site of what once was the Trenton Marine Terminal on the Delaware River. This terminal was important to the seagoing traffic in the 1930s and 1940s when Trenton was a major port. Today, the site is important as a major recreation area.

To transform this industrial site into a recreation area, the designers had to overcome certain problems. One of the major problems was that the historic artifacts (e.g. gantry cranes and cargo masts) had to be incorporated into the design. These magnificent reminders of the shipping activity along the Delaware have been left in place and turned into active

play equipment. The railing is another element in the park that speaks of the "industrial archeology" of the setting. Precast concrete bollards linked with steel cables provides a railing reminiscent of a ship's rail. Benches are provided behind this railing, looking out over the Delaware. The railing is positioned so that the view is unobstructed, and a wooden boardwalk (a New Jersey tradition) between a double row of plane trees and a border of crushed stone run the length of the park.

Recalling the state's numerous ocean communities, a Marine Center is another vital focus of the park. A marina is a part

of this center that offers launching facilities, boat rentals and nautical supplies. A farmer's market, shops and food service facilities are included in future development plans.

Thus far, the strength of this development is in the simplicity with which the designers worked with the industrial ambiance and the heavy industrial equipment of the past. The 70-foot cargo masts and the World War I gantry cranes stand as unadorned, elegant, giant sculptures — a testimony to their former glory. The play sculpture integrated into this industrial portion of the site is an imaginative touch that forges a connection between the past uses of the site and its present recreational character.

In a sense, this park is more than a recreational area, it's also a museum. With the world and technology changing so rapidly, it's important to preserve remnants of the past to measure our progress. This park is a first step in Trenton's redevelopment of the waterfront. The promising progress made here is a benchmark for the future revitalization of the entire waterfront area.

Project
Trenton Marine Terminal Park
Location
Trenton, New Jersey, USA
Client
New Jersey Economic Development Authority
Design Firm
Arnold Associates, Landscape Architects
Photographer
Henry F. Arnold, Janet Gnall
Consultant
Arthur Lutzker, Architect

Juxtapositions

The TRANSPOTOMAC CANAL CENTER, a collaboration of M. Paul Friedberg and the sculptors Anne and Patrick Poirier, is located on the Potomac River in Alexandria, Virginia. This installation funded by a private concern (Savage Fogarty) for the public good, is a play of the formal and informal, restrained and exuberant, conventional with the unconventional. Further contrast is supplied in the informal birch plantings and the artful naturalness of the landscaping.

The playfulness of sculptural forms seems reminiscent of antiquity, while at the same time it appears to be Daliesque and surreal in context. One is never quite sure

whether whimsy or history has the final say, here, except perhaps in the design of the force and play of the water. In this there seems to be no ambiguity. Water is the powerful force, water is never static, never quite controlled. Watching the interplay of the water perhaps one senses the high flood plain of the Potomac River.

The source of the water in the design is a 30-foot high bronze arrow thrust into the ground. The effect is that the arrow has pierced the ground and brought forth the water — a classic interpretation from

antiquity. The water cascades down the steep grades through formal pools, spewing mouths, blind eyes, into a grotto at the foot of horseshoe stairs. Into this grotto have "fallen" random sculptural fragments. One wonders if these have been left behind. Perhaps they've fallen from the sky. The source is left undefined. But just beyond is definition in the angular amphitheater punctuated by the obelisk at the river's edge. One can see the inspiration of the obelisk — the Washington Monument — across the river. Reverence or humor?

This formal axis from the huge bronze spear to the 14-ton marble obelisk is called the "Promenade Classique" and leads the visitor down a series of levels to the riverfront promenade. From this vantage point one looks up into the eyes of giants sitting on pillars surveying the comings and goings of mere mortals as the eyes of the vanquished look up from their watery grave. Such is the fantasy of the moment in this installation of the surreal. The sense of scale accounts for much of the mood of this installation. And

the sense of scale is heightened by the integration of the sculptural elements with the landscape design.

In his conception of the design, M. Paul Friedberg wanted sculpture that would be "absorbed" into the design. In this he succeeded magnificently. There is no area in this design where one can stand back and survey the sculptural monument sited so perfectly in the viewing space. In the Transpotomac Canal Center the sculpture is all around you. As you leave you are aware it has even permeated your consciousness.

Project
Transpotomac Canal Center
Location
Alexandria, Virginia, USA
Client
Savage/Fogarty
Design Firm
M. Paul Friedberg
Sculptors
Anne and Patrick Poirier
Photographer
Ron Green

The Jewel of Battery Park
A Japanese Garden On Stilts

The interplay of coiling and undulating spaces — *SOUTH COVE* — at Battery Park City is a collaboration of three talented individuals: *Mary Miss*, site artist; *Stanton Eckstut*, architect; and *Susan Child*, landscape architect. Stanton Eckstut, who in his former partnership (Cooper & Eckstut) did the masterplanning for the complex, essentially did the planning and design for the straight, orderly, historically oriented Esplanade. He also contributed this vision of historical integrity, integration and continuity to this termination of the Esplanade — South Cove.

Susan Child further elaborated on this use of the indigenous and historically correct in her choice of plant materials — trees, grasses and wild rushes that reflect the ecology of a cove on the Atlantic seaboard. She also contributed her knowledge of the characteristic forms of coves and how they are formed in nature. Within these parameters of formality, history, ecology and the natural

environment of river and shoreline, Mary Miss added (or integrated) the organic, ever flowing multi-layers of this pedestrian space.

The installation takes much from the Japanese in character and flavor, from the colors to the choice and placement of materials. The rocks, the ever-present boulders that seem so randomly placed (as if they were there originally and the designers built the project around them), were carefully situated by a crane operator directed by Mary Miss. In keeping with the true spirit of the Japanese garden, the idea here is to intensify nature.

Another idea expressed here seems to be the intensification of the sense of play, of enjoyment of the waterfront, the city, the historic legacy of the site and the "sense of place." The sense of place, of course, is the water — the Hudson River, the view of the Statue of Liberty, the edge of danger that any transition between earth and water engenders. All of this is expressed in the final execution. The calm, orderly Esplanade gives way subtly to the cove space, the pavers give way to metal

169

grilles, which give way to boardwalk, which gives way to the water. On the metal grilles you seem suspended over the water. One false step and you would sink beneath the surface.

Such is the essence of South Cove. You feel you are never truly separate from the water. You feel closer to the river here than at any place on the Esplanade. Definitions are vague, barriers are drawn fine and extended to the limit. The pair of metal staircases that swirl up to the lookout post are topped by a crown shape reminiscent of the Statue of Liberty. From this vantage point the statue is visible and the river, the ever present water, is seen from another level. Levels are ever-changing in this three-acre space. Levels define areas, create unusual and provocative experiences, and always remind you of the changing rise and fall of the tides and the river.

Perhaps the success of this space can be attributed to that concept. Each of the designers sensed and used the river as a guidepost, a litmus paper. Each was concerned that the visitor, the participant in the space, be aware of and use the river. When one studies the final forms

and organic sequences it is with a feeling of delight and mystery. Whatever fantasy it provokes in the visitor, the feeling is nautical, from the sapphire blue lights that delineate the pier, to the pilings, to the free-standing square arches and the seawall which marks the rise and fall of the tides.

Project
South Cove
Location
Battery Park City, New York, New York, USA
Client
Battery Park City Authority
Artist
Mary Miss
Architect
Stan Eckstut
Landscape Architect
Susan Child

In Celebration of a River

Landscape architects *Haruto Kobayashi and Ikuya Nishikaw + TLA* collaborated in the design of the *SUISHA (WATER MILL) PARK* in Yotsuba 1-chome, Itabashi-ku, Tokyo. The symbolism and significance of the park is taken from the Maeyatsu River which is the major source of water (both potable and irrigation water) for the Itabashi ward.

Although the river provides the theme of the park, most residents have no visual connection with the riverbed itself. The Maeyatsu River has its source west of the Itabashi ward in Akatsuka. As it flows through the ward, the river runs through a

culvert hidden underneath the road. Yet this river, this source of life for people and plants, is deeply ingrained in the lives of the inhabitants. Perhaps this lack of visual connection is the reason for the symbolic reference to the river in the design of the park.

The park is skillfully designed to symbolize the river and take advantage of the natural conditions of the site. The site is long and narrow, interrupted by a road, and slopes east to west. There are four

"zones" or areas on the site, some dictated by geology, some by existing water sources (the stream), some by existing vegetation and some by existing traffic patterns — the roads. One can enter the park from a number of points and proceed to the experience of choice, or one can begin sequentially at either end — the Water Mill Zone or the Tea House Zone — and work toward the center of the park where the Limpid Stream Zone and the Mountain Village Zone are on either side of the Entry Square.

The Limpid Stream zone symbolizes the source of the river with the natural

geographic conditions creating a scaled-down version of high mountains and a waterfall (30 meters high) as the focal element. The scale of the components is consistent, and only by introducing human scale can the miniaturization be realized.

The Mountain Village Zone has been created in existing vegetation and contains a charcoal-burning shed to lend credence to the fantasy. The Water Mill Zone and Tea House Zone are the more "civilized" installations, each providing open space and architectural elements.

The Tea House Zone, a spare area covered with moss, also provides the

traditional Japanese Garden elements complete with "dry landscape garden" — the Karesansui. There is a heart-shaped pond with a small island and a Waiting Arbor and Resting Shed. The Tea House contains a Shoin (large study room) and several smaller rooms. The whole of the Tea House Zone is used for international exchange and social education. In fact,

the whole park seems like an educational experience.

This carefully constructed symbolic design that educates the inhabitants about the sources of their un-seen Maeyatsu River, is a contribution to ecological and social education for both the visitor and citizen of this area of Tokyo.

Project
Suisha (Water Mill) Park
Location
Tokyo, Japan
Client
Tokamaru-Ishikawa Land Readjustment Association and Itabashi Ward
Design Firm
Tokyo Landscape Architects Inc.,
Haruto Kobayashi
Photographer
© Tokyo Landscape Architects Inc.,
Haruto Kobayashi

Accommodating the Growth of the City

In Sendai City in Japan, planners are involved in incorporating new elements of growth and progress — for example, the construction of a subway system — while at the same time, retaining as many elements as possible of their park system. To modify *KOTODAI PARK*, landscape architects *Haruto Kobayashi + TLA* have been commissioned to take advantage of the opportunity for refurbishment and rearrangement that this disruption allows.

The theme of the modification is to establish the park as a new place for recreation and relaxation. In addition, the modification establishes Sendai City as a "green" city. Plant materials and garden areas are foreseen as hallmarks for the future. One of the problems in this modification, however, is the fact that the site of the park is broken into three separate areas because of the national highway and city streets that pierce the site from both axes.

The subway construction, of course, presents still another problem. Entrances and exits were to be built into the existing park space. How to integrate these new subway access passages was an issue. The designers solved the dilemma by incorporating these elements into the

redesign of the park. Each entrance and exit focus was transformed into a plaza-like space that could handle the crowds and confusion that would ensue during rush hour. The sidewalks of the highway and city roads were also incorporated into the redesign, acting as directional elements for the park as a whole. To unify the three separate areas, the same materials and design motifs were used throughout all three parts.

The stark, controlled sense of the design with the carefully articulated steps, the fountain area punched through the paving, and the carefully manicured lawn areas seem to be signatures of the design style of this park. These elements create a sense of open space and tranquility in an urban atmosphere. This, perhaps, is achieved by the concentrations of paved area as opposed to planted, green area. One offsets the other. The sense of new construction does not exist in this re-design. Rather, one feels that the redesign is simply an evolution of an existing park, one that will grow with the technological changes and needs of the population of Sendai City.

Project
Kotodai Park
Location
Sendai City, Japan
Client
Park Section, Sendai City
Design Firm
Tokyo Landscape Architects Inc.,
Haruto Kobayashi
Photographer
©Tokyo Landscape Architects Inc.,
Haruto Kobayashi

CHAPTER V

Inspirational & Historic Spaces

A Legacy for the Future

Edmund. *Thou, nature, art my goddess; to thy law.*
My services are bound

King Lear, Act 1, scene 2; William Shakespeare

Monuments are one way in which the cultures of past civilizations have been transmitted to us. How would we have learned of the Celtic culture if all the great megaliths had been destroyed? Certainly not by the written word. Even if a culture left a written record, as the Greeks did, would a description of the temples have been as vivid, as elucidating as seeing remnants of the actual building? Nothing is quite so descriptive as the actual site, construction or object — even millennia later.

One might ask, did the citizens of ancient cultures design and build these monuments we now see as educational and inspirational so that we of the future would know of their existence? One can't possibly know. Certainly, it's a factor that is considered today in the design of monuments and other elements that we consider the legacies of our civilization — the commemoration of what society considers worthy of recognition. Considering the import of monuments that have been constructed in the past 20 years, in both Western and Eastern cultures, makes one thoughtful. Monuments often commemorate fallen warriors in the never-ending battles of our planet. Perhaps that has been true throughout history.

PAST & FUTURE IN TERMS OF THE PRESENT

The different categories of this chapter — National Parks & Geographic Wonders, Monuments & Memorials, Cemeteries, Sculpture Gardens, Meditative Spaces — are concerned with all the aspects of time. History is first aspect of time we deal with in this chapter. Most of us enjoy a visit to a historical site, to learn from ancient cultures and to experience the novelty of spaces and objects from the past. Some of us close our eyes and try to imagine just what it really was like 3,000 years ago when that image was carved into the hill, or that cave was inhabited.

What does the designer have to do

with something created so long ago? Surely he or she isn't going to redesign this historic monument! Surely, however, sensitive designers are needed to maintain and protect this historic monument from visitors and environmental damage. It's not an easy task to design and integrate an element so that it appears at first glance, at least, that nothing has been altered and the site is still in pristine condition after hundreds or thousands of years. One might say that to preserve the past for the future takes a very light touch.

Geographic wonders, such as the Rosh Hanikra Sea Caves in Israel, are another kind of national park. Maintaining and developing the sites of natural wonders is a delicate balancing act. It's important that visitors be able to access the site in order to enjoy the marvel of nature. But, it is equally as important for the visitor not to alter or damage the delicate ecological balance of the site. It is a challenge that also takes a designer with a light touch. When visiting sites of this kind, it's important that man not leave a record of his visitation.

A RECORD OF OUR HOPES & DREAMS
Other records are important to leave. We design and build monuments and memorials as records of those who have died. We want to create a remembrance of a person or an event to serve as a reminder of the past and a remembrance for future generations.

Cemeteries are still another form of monuments and memorials, only they exist in a private rather than a public context. They differ from monuments and memorials in their siting and location — all private monuments and memorials in a cemetery exist in a concentrated area set aside for this use. The forms of cemeteries also differ, from the quiet churchyard of the Christian tradition to the "Cities of the Dead" in Cairo.

One form that memorials, monuments and cemeteries share, however, is that they generally occupy space, and in some cases, green space. In our over-populated planet it might be an added benefit that the places we select for burying our dead also provide us with space, plants, sunlight and a chance for quiet meditation when we visit the gravesites of our loved ones.

THE NEED FOR QUIET
Sculpture Gardens and Meditative Spaces are designed to provide a place for contemplation. In a sculpture garden, the contemplation of the man-made beauty of the sculpture is on an equal plane with the contemplation of the natural elements of the garden — plants, water, rock, earth and the like. The successful sculpture garden, of course, would so integrate the artwork with nature that each would serve as a foil for the other and the two elements would enhance each other.

Meditative spaces are perhaps harder to define and illustrate. Some of the examples shown here — a Japanese garden on a rooftop or a lookout over the Mediterranean — may seem too diverse and arbitrary. Each has been chosen, however, because it appears to be a place designed for meditation and repose — a place to look outward and inward simultaneously. The external natural elements are used as a stimulus to evoke calm. In our chaotic world such places are rare. Perhaps the time to use and enjoy these spaces is even rarer.

In Inspirational & Historic Spaces passive rather than active use of time is inherent. When one visits the various sites and spaces portrayed, one is not called upon to engage in activities or forms of play, or even to interact with others unless one chooses. These sites are places to be a spectator and observer; the interaction is with oneself, the landscape and time — past, present and future.

Interdependency & World Heritage

On a site designated by UNESCO as a world heritage site, the designers of *The LeBlond Partnership Architects & Planners* (architects) and *Carson McCulloch Associates Ltd.* (landscape architects) created a massive, seven-level structure that has a minimum impact on the environment. One might say that the designers achieved an interdependency between the complex, the natural contours and the existing rock outcroppings. Keeping the site intact and building a

facility that would be visually unobtrusive were, of course, part of the program requirements for the *HEAD-SMASHED-IN BUFFALO JUMP INTERPRETIVE CENTRE (ESTIPAH-SIKIKINI-KOTS)* in Alberta, Canada.

Communal hunting was practiced on this 5,700-year-old site by four prehistoric cultures; it is the best preserved and largest jump site in North America. The prehistoric plains people would round up the buffalo, pasture them in a gathering basin at Olsen Creek, then drive them through "drive lines" (marked with rock cairns) to the top of a 300-meter sandstone cliff. The buffalo plunged 11 meters to their death. Usually this "jump" would provide enough food for a year. The resulting deposits at the base of the cliff (more than 10 meters deep) have yielded, and continue to yield, a wealth of artifacts for archeologists. To take advantage of this, archeological research laboratories and exhibition space are on the bottom level of the complex near the ongoing archeological dig.

The entrance is also on the bottom level. Using a series of elevators and stairs visitors emerge to the top of the site to walk (with a sense of precariousness) along the cliff top to the jump site. The sense of precariousness comes, in part, because the building is virtually invisible from this vantage point. This is one of the many successful aspects of the design. Sod (cut from the surrounding plain) covers the roof of the majority of the structure and great care has been taken to insure that the grass planted on the roof matches the adjacent natural landscape.

Care has also been taken to match the concrete shell and retaining walls with the indigenous sandstone. There is a story told that when the Elders of the Peigan Indians came to perform the ceremonial rituals to bless the building as a sacred place, they (who possessed the eyes and wisdom of the eagle) passed the building twice — and couldn't find it. From a distance it does appear to be a part of the cliff, so carefully have the designers worked to achieve integration. Even the parking has been made inconspicuous from the approach road.

The original contours of the building site have been replaced and the subsequent landscape reclamation and development sought to re-vegetate the site to approximate the existing adjacent plant materials. Another goal was to integrate pathways and other directional and access elements into the natural environment with a minimum of disruption.

This, of course, is one of the ongoing problems on a site with continuous visitors. Control of crowds in an existing landscape is mandatory. On this site, paths have been carefully planned and guides take the visitors on their journey.

The journey here at Head-Smashed-In Buffalo Jump Interpretive Centre ("head-smashed-in" refers to a young brave who hid at the base of the cliff and was smashed between the sandstone and the buffalo) is into the past, into a long vanished culture and forgotten way of life. The voyagers of the present are not always cognizant of the fragility of the past, nor how to preserve it for future generations. On this site the designers have taken great care and have exercised enormous creativity to allow glimpses and participation by those so inclined. At the same time, they have protected the stark, awesome beauty of this windswept, imposing site.

Project
Head-Smashed-In Buffalo Jump
Interpretive Centre
Location
Alberta, Canada
Client
Alberta Public Works Supply Services
Design Firm
The LeBlond Partnership Architects and Planners: Robert H. LeBlond, partner and designer
Landscape Design
Carson McCulloch Associates Ltd., Gary Carson
Photographer
Robert H. LeBlond
Awards
1990 Governor General Award of Canada for Architecture; 1989 Pacific Cultural Heritage Award; 1988 Award of Excellence for the use of Concrete in Alberta (American Concrete Institute); 1988 Award of Excellence for Design and Construction in Concrete (Portland Cement Association)

In Reverence of a Tree

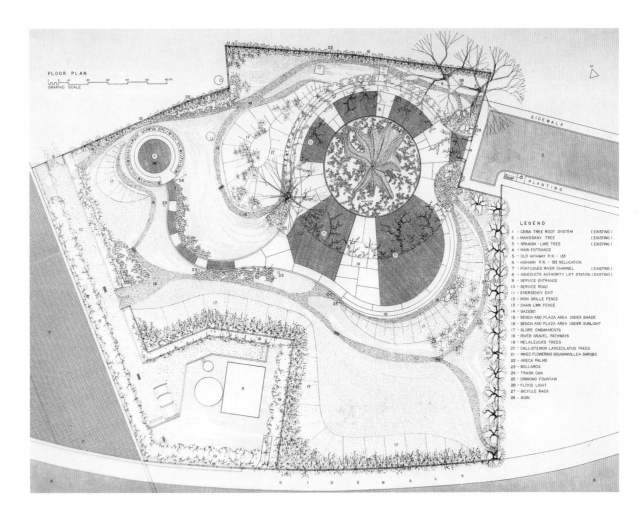

To say that *CEIBA TREE PARK* in Ponce, Puerto Rico, was created so that inhabitants and visitors could worship this 100-year-old magnificent *Ceiba petandra* tree might be overstating the case, but certainly this tree is considered to be an important cultural, if not natural resource to the inhabitants of the island.

When *Jorge del Rio* designed this park as a facility where the tree can be admired and enjoyed, his main concern was to create a space where all vistas and sight lines focused on the tree. He wanted to protect the tree, but at the same time allow the public to walk around, view the tree from different angles, and perhaps even "feel a part of this magnificent specimen." The flowing circularity of his design seems to accomplish all this.

The large circular enclosure for the tree itself — the crown is approximately one hundred feet in diameter — becomes the focal point of the design. The surrounding paving, in random colored concrete pavers used in conjunction with concrete paving, create both a walk around the tree and a mini-plaza which forms a directional element leading to the gazebo and other parts of the park.

The gazebo (a traditional element of the townscape in rural Puerto Rico) provides both shelter from passing storms when necessary and also a space for sitting, picnicking or passive games. It also gives a definition to the space in a form reminiscent of the crown of the tree. In effect it is the needed accent for this

sinuous park space that defines the large tree element as being dominant. The sinuous flow and movement of the plan seems to symbolize the growth and pattern of the tree from its root system to its branch system. The lush, flowing tropical planting also seems to emphasize the fecundity of both the revered tree and the surrounding natural vegetation of Puerto Rico.

In effect, that is what this park setting is attempting to express. This magnificent tree has been growing unchecked for over a hundred years, partly because the population of Ponce protected it and made it into a traditional site. True, the climate of Puerto Rico may encourage this type of growth and vegetation, but in today's world, the reverence and protection of one specimen tree is not an everyday occurrence. As the result of Jorge del Rio's care in creating site conditions necessary for a healthy tree, however, this specimen tree and the surrounding plantings will hopefully continue for another hundred years.

Project
Ceiba Tree Park
Location
Ponce, Puerto Rico
Client
U.S. Corps of Engineers; Commonwealth of Puerto Rico Department of Natural Resources and the Commonwealth of Puerto Rico Department of Sports and Recreation
Design Firm
Jorge del Rio, FAIA, Architect and Planner
Design Team
Jorge del Rio, FAIA, project and landscape design; Eduardo Lopez, AIA, project coordination; John Lauwaert, master plan design; Bob Bullock, Yamil Castillo, engineers; Samuel Perez, working drawings; Maria Zayas, project administration
Photographers
Francisco Vando; floor plan by Pedro Martinez
Consultants
Leonardo Vidal, Luis Capestany, David McCloskey, engineers
Awards
1989 Merit Award Landscape Architecture, Chief of Engineers Design and Environmental Awards Program; 1989 URBE Award in Architectural Excellence, The Puerto Rico Academy of Arts, History and Archaeology

187

Problems of Accessibility

The history of the grottos at *ROSH HANIKRA* is one of caravans and armies — a passage point between Lebanon, Syria, Palestine, Egypt, and the rest of North Africa. The Old Testament refers to Misraphot Mayim (south of Rosh Hanikra) as a border settlement of the Israelites. Alexander of Macedonia (323 B.C.E.) is supposed to have hewn a tunnel at this crucial juncture to create a passage for his army after his siege of Tire. Drawings from the period also show stairways carved into the rock. During the First World War the British Army constructed a road, and during the Second World War they dug a railway tunnel 250 meters long for shipping supplies from Egypt to Beirut.

The attempt at easy access, the passage between countries through the tunnels, highways and stairways, came to an end in March 1948 during Israel's War for Independence. The Palmach blew up the railway bridges in the grottos to prevent an invasion by the Lebanese army. Security for the new State of Israel was provided (Rosh Hanikra is at the border between Israel and Lebanon), but access to the beauty and majesty of these caverns carved by the sea from the limestone hills was lost.

To allow the public to experience these magnificent sea caves, the firm of Miller-Blum was retained to develop a proposal that would allow public access to these exquisite spaces. Twelve alternate proposals were presented. From these creative ideas came the decision to install a cable car to provide vertical access and circulation on the face of the cliff. Horizontal circulation in the grottos was a more difficult task. To provide pedestrian circulation within these spaces, essentially still a part of the sea, a plan was developed that would allow both a surface trail and an underground trail. In addition, selected portions of the cave areas were blasted out by carefully controlled explosions to enlarge these natural wonders and make them more accessible to visitors. Experienced mining engineers were used for this process.

To control visitors in the grottos themselves, steps, walks, railings and lighting were installed. Care was taken in this installation to ensure that all introduced elements were integrated into the natural setting to enhance and heighten the dramatic experience without detracting in any way from the sea-sculpted surfaces. These mammoth spaces can also be entered via the water by boat or by diving. To enter in this fashion would produce an entirely different experience from the pedestrian entry. Certainly a diver entering the cave and being able to see

above and below the water could create a totality of sensual stimulation.

In effect that's what the "pattern of flow" is intended to do. Descending the stark white cliff face in the cable car, suspended in space, entering the dark grottos with the sea crashing at your feet, walking over surf-slick rocks — all these myriad experiences are bound to alter your perceptions of earth, sky and water. Perhaps when you return, when your sky chariot deposits you once again on the top of the cliff, you will return with a sense of reverence for the power of nature and man's ability to alter it.

Project
Rosh Hanikra
Location
Israel
Client
Sulam-Tzor Regional Council
Design Firm
Miller-Blum Environmental Planning
Mining Engineer
M. Navias
Project Leader
D. Jaegle, S. Heimann

Agriculture + Recreation

The owners of the Compton Beauchamp Estates hired *Colvin and Moggridge*, Landscape Architects, to redesign the setting of *WHITE HORSE HILL* (the highest point on Berkshire Downs) before turning it over to the National Trust, the present owners. Their desire was to preserve this historic area — both the site and the ambiance — in perpetuity.

At the time of the restoration, the preservation of the monument was in jeopardy. Erosion was one of the major problems; the famous earthworks of White Horse and Uffington Castle were badly overused more than a decade ago. In addition, farmland was in competition with the monument site and the parking was

both inadequate and unsightly. Solving the erosion problem, of course, was more complex than the re-siting of the car park.

In order to keep the monuments from being overrun and overused by the increasing number of visitors, the designers decided to increase the recreation area on the Downs from 35 to 230 acres. In order to do this, they had to reclaim ploughed land and reinstate grassland. This reclaimed area was "regrassed" with a seed mix designed for the following: 1) to match the color of the old turf; 2) to

achieve an open sward that would allow for herb species from the old chalk turf to re-colonize the area; 3) to provide adequate grazing for the sheep. Grazing Sheep were a primary ingredient in the health of this reclaimed land.

The opening up of the grasslands allowed more recreational space for the visitor seeking to play on the free, high downland, thus, hopefully, creating less stress and play on the monuments themselves. To achieve this relationship, the siting of this area was carefully chosen and extremely important. Visitors can see the White Horse from the grass downland, but accessibility is achieved only after a rather considerable hike. Only those with

the stamina and willpower to make this hike will play on the monument. The re-siting of the car park was also a major factor in freeing the monuments from over use.

The original car park provided easy access to both Uffington Castle and the White Horse. This area has been reduced in size, and 20 spaces have been provided, only for disabled visitors. The new car park has been installed (and hidden from site) in an old existing chalk pit along a perimeter road. Although local residents objected to this distant relocation on the grounds that they had "immemorial rights of car access," permission was obtained. This new car park was carefully constructed to allow site lines to both Uffington Castle and the White Horse, and is a gravel space planted with beech and pine trees.

Beech trees are indigenous to this site and were here before the advent of man. Man, of course, created this site, but long before the Romans came in 54 A.D. Other than those facts, the history of these earthworks remains mysterious. Perhaps that is one of the reasons this area is so provocative. Another reason may be the fact that the White Horse seems constructed to be seen from the sky rather than the land. This aspect has puzzled both archaeologists and historians, and drawn the curious who come hoping to solve the riddle. Colvin and Moggridge

hoped not to solve this riddle, but rather to protect and preserve the secrets for cogitation by future generations. They have skillfully redesigned this space to accomplish this. Even if the visitors who come unceasingly by automobile do not seek to experience these historic sights from the air, the new design allows them to view them from sufficient distance that the impact is greater than when trying to capture the whole from a too-intimate view.

Project
White Horse Hill
Location
Berkshire Downs, Uffington, Oxfordshire, England
Client
The Hon. David Astor (subsequently donated to the National Trust)
Design Firm
Colvin and Moggridge: Hal Moggridge, James Riley
Photographer
David McQuitty
Consultants
Hugh Preston - Knight Frank & Rutley, agent; Rendel Palmer & Tritton, road engineering
Awards
1987 Europa Nostra Diploma of Merit; 1987 BBC Design Awards Finalist

For Those Who Died

Palimpsestos - rubbed smooth to write again, history written over and over again on the same ancient ground. The monument is a palimpsest.

The harsh but beautiful landscape across the soldiers fought and died has, since the beginning, contrasted with man's artifacts of civilization, cultivation and war. Man has destroyed and so has time. But the antiquities in this landscape symbolize man's spirit as well as his struggles with nature and his own land. The most noble monument to man's spirit is the doric column. The most futile is the rusting, shell-torn fragment of modern conflict. These pieces emerge from the ground, implying vast buried relics of both civilization and conflict. This ground is the most placid of places, an amphitheatre of seats where an audience contemplates this Greek tragedy. Like an ancient glade, the arc of seats resides in an olive grove and the formal cypresses stand evidence of a sacred place. The names of ancient and modern battles are inscribed in the faces of the amphitheatre. Various scales contrast — the column is oversized and cut by clear imagination, not the wear of time. The rocks, as sharp as flint, are also seen as mountains. A mosaic pavement is the map of the peninsula and archipelago of Greece, on which this haunting ensemble resides.

This "competition statement" was submitted with the winning design for the *AUSTRALIAN/HELLENIC MEMORIAL* in Canberra, Australia, by *Ancher Mortlock and Woolley*. The designers of this memorial, *Ken Woolley and Wally Barda*, prepared this statement to explain the diverse and provocative symbolism of their submission to this limited competition for architects and sculptors sponsored by the NCDC. Their submission, of course, won the competition, and the judges were so impressed with their statement that it was inscribed on one of the plaques of the memorial. The other of the two plaques carries a Greek inscription that states who the memorial commemorates — those who died in the campaign for Crete, at sea in the Mediterranean, members of other branches (including nurses) of the armed forces and Greek civilians who helped Australians — from World Wars I and II. The overall concept of the memorial is the "universal destruction over history of symbols of civilization and cultivation by war and by time."

The two primary symbols erupting from this circular ringed site are the oversized doric column and the twisted steel columns from a wrecked building in Sydney (further damaged by gunfire, as requested by the designers, by the Australian Army). These

symbols of the classic past and the hostile present make one aware of the ever-present nature of conflict among nations, and the inability of man to form stable governments and peaceful alliances. The plantings on this site are also symbolic and evocative.

Cypress and olive trees are the predominant plantings. The cypress trees are meant to symbolize the sacredness of the site, but cypress branches also symbolize mourning, perhaps suggesting a dual symbolism. Olive trees are used as an element of an ancient glade, but, again, olive branches are symbols of peace; the olive tree has been an important food source since ancient times — multiple symbolism. Perhaps, this was the aim, focus and desire of the designers.

To symbolize in a coherent manner, in solid form, all the forces that contribute to war, conflict and destruction is an awesome task. Further, to do this on a site that already incorporates several war

memorials and is a "parade ground," an area perhaps designed to show off troops and military might, further complicates the task. The impact of this memorial seems to be contemplation — contemplation of the impact and cost of conflict as opposed to the glories and contributions of civilization. One senses, perhaps, an ambiguity with the site. On the other hand, is there a better place to erect a monument that will cause people to consider the long range effects of their actions?

Project
Australian/Hellenic Memorial
Location
Canberra, Australia
Client
National Capital Development Commission
Design Firm
Ancher Mortlock & Woolley Pty. Ltd.: Kenneth Woolley, concept and design control; Wally Barda, design collaborator
Photographer
Kenneth Woolley

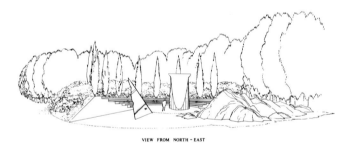

VIEW FROM NORTH - EAST

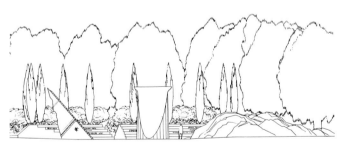

SECTION B-B

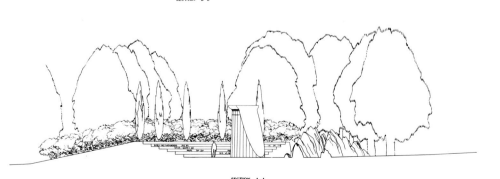

SECTION A-A

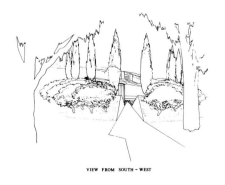

VIEW FROM SOUTH - WEST

Commemorating a Pioneer

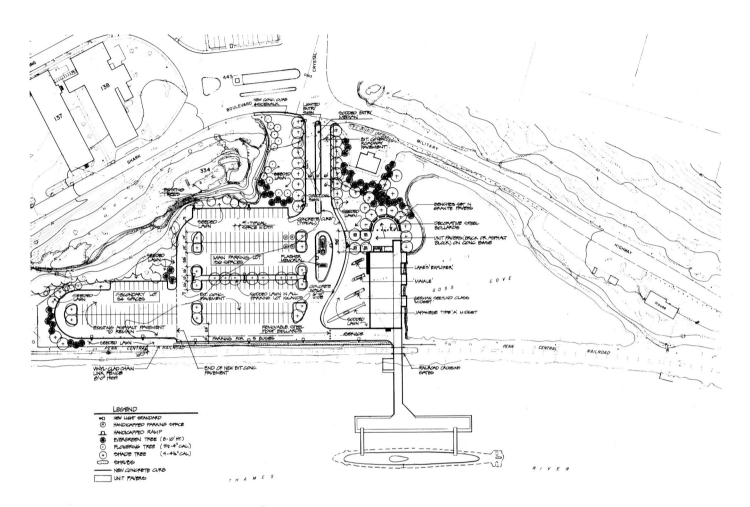

Cambridge Seven Associates, Inc. (architects) and *Carol R. Johnson & Associates* (landscape architects) collaborated in the siting and design of the *USS NAUTILUS SUBMARINE FORCE LIBRARY & MUSEUM* at Groton, Connecticut. This site, adjacent to naval and industrial facilities instrumental in the design, construction and active use of this first nuclear submarine, is a salt-water tidal cove on the Thames River. Across the river is the U.S. Merchant Marine Academy.

The raison d'être for this site and structure, of course, is the USS Nautilus itself, now a ship on the Historic Register. This submarine has been decommissioned and retrofitted for this exhibit, and lies berthed in the water off a pier behind the museum itself. A walkway and viewing area with railings reminiscent of a ship's railing lead to the boat. Four other

submarines — miniatures by contrast — are situated out of water on pedestals and concrete pads incorporated into the lawn area.

Lawn is a predominant theme on this flat site. The small shrubs and trees that have been introduced (bayberry, beach plum, rugosa rose, Japanese black pine, Australian pine, oak, ash, rhododendron) are all plant materials that can survive adjacent to a salt-water environment. The plantings are also meant to soften this site, which had little or no significant vegetation to begin with. The trees were also introduced as directional elements and to focus the eye on the exhibited elements. These elements include the giant steel circular arch that represents a structural rib from the hull framing of a submarine. This dramatic entry component

forces the visitor to recognize the scale of the commemorative craft by walking through the arch. The stark siting of this elegant element reinforces the experience.

Starkness is the primary impression of this museum and site. Starkness, in this connotation, is not pejorative. The sea has a starkness, an unforgivingness about it. This submarine — perhaps all submarines — conveys a sleek, sinister starkness. The site, in this sense, is appropriate. The cliffs and rock outcroppings at the landward side of the site perhaps also contribute to this feeling.

There is no lush fecundity to this installation, to this riverfront site. There is almost the impression that the plant materials struggle to grow against the winds, against the elements. One senses control and discipline in the design — the same control and discipline exercised by those who designed, constructed and manned this now historic craft.

Project
USS Nautilus Memorial Submarine Force Library and Museum
Location
Groton, Connecticut, USA
Client
Department of the Navy, Northern Division
Design Firm
Cambridge Seven Associates Inc.: G.W. Terry Rankine, FAIA; John Stebbins, AIA; John Merkler, AIA; Robert Galloway; Mark Hammer, AIA
Landscape Architects
Carol R. Johnson & Associates: Carol Johnson, Randy Sorenson, Harry Fuller
Photographer
Nick Wheeler
Consultants
Weidlinger Associates, Inc.; Fay Spofford & Thorndike, Inc.; Howard Brandston Lighting Design
Awards
1987 Excellence in Architecture, AIA/ New England Regional Council; 1987 Boston Exports Award for Excellence, Boston Society of Architects; 1986 Distinguished Architectural Achievement, AIA/Naval Facilities Engineering Command

Guardian of the Old City

DAVID'S TOWER stands at the entrance of the Old City of Jerusalem. The tower and citadel are part of the historic wall that surrounds the old city. This site was neglected (parts of it had been destroyed) until the unification of Jerusalem in 1967 when the landscape architects of Miller-Blum were retained to restore the site. Their overall concept was to divide the area into two levels — upper and lower.

The lower level is the path that runs along the wall. The stone pavers ramp down a few feet to this level and allow the visitor — as he or she walks adjacent to the crenelated battlements — to experience this wall as part of the citadel, part of an historic line of defense. Lowering the level by ramping rather than by steps and walls allows both levels to flow into one another and to be part of the totality of the design.

The upper level forms the principal part of the design. Here the designers were concerned with creating a plaza area, which, in their view, should serve several functions: a panoramic observation point; an entrance to the citadel and museum; a public garden; and a site for public gatherings and official functions. The designers also wanted the design and the materials used in the plaza to be as unpretentious as possible and not detract from the grandeur of this historic buildings. To accomplish this, they went to the patterns of the Old City's paved areas for inspiration.

The size, type, angles and alignment of the paving in the Old City were studied and analyzed to provide the designers with models from which to draw their inspiration. Color and texture were also

important. Care had to be taken to articulate the new paving in ways to define and separate it from the ancient structures, while at the same time, the new had to be integrated with the old. Using similar materials of compatible color and texture created a space that feels whole. The installations may have occurred at different times in the historical time line, but in the feel of time and place the parts recognize each other.

This sensitive design will also allow the recognition and integration to increase over time. The paving stones were laid with soil instead of cement mortar. As time passes, grass will sprout between the stones, giving focus to the ancient stones and walls and the panoramic view over the Western part of Jerusalem.

Project
David's Tower
Location
Jerusalem, Israel
Client
Jerusalem Municipality
Design Firm
Miller-Blum Environmental Planning

Chilling Reflections

...UNTIL JUSTICE ROLLS DOWN LIKE WATERS AND RIGHTEOUSNESS LIKE A MIGHTY STREAM

MARTIN LUTHER KING, JR.

When a board member asked *Maya Lin* to design a memorial on the plaza of the new Southern Poverty Law Center (designed by Cole & Hill) in Montgomery, Alabama, she broke her promise to herself never to design another memorial. She said, "I felt very fortunate for being asked to participate in another major turning point for our country." This memorial commemorating a "turning point," is the *CIVIL RIGHTS MEMORIAL.* Located on the plaza as requested, this simple composition of two forms and a reflecting pool leads the visitor into the Center, while at the same time, provoking and proclaiming both the courage and the cowardice of the past.

The quotation from Dr. Martin Luther King, Jr., "...Until justice rolls down like waters and righteousness like a mighty stream.", inscribed on the 9-foot-high curving Canadian black granite wall was the inspiration for Lin. Water is a central design element in this memorial. The concept of water as justice, rolling, is evident in all facets of the design. The central element of the design, the cantilevered 11-foot-6-inch-disk, also of Canadian black granite, however, is the most powerful statement.

The power of this form, of course, could come from the hovering, tangential quality of the cantilever. There is the feeling of substance and strength, but also the feeling of a form resting, touching, and yet poised for flight: a form in transition. The names inscribed on the surface of the disk — names of those who died in the struggle for civil rights, are constantly washed by water bubbling from the center, running over the face and dripping down onto the pavement below.

Reading the names, watching the slow subtle movement of the water, one also

sees one's own face reflected onto the surface, mingling with the names of the dead. In a sense, that's what gives this memorial power. No visitor can read the names and not — however fleetingly — be a part of the vision on the surface of the disk.

Project
Civil Rights Memorial
Location
Montgomery, Alabama, USA
Client
Southern Poverty Law Center
Artist
Maya Lin
Photographer
© Maya Lin

207

A Cleft in the Earth

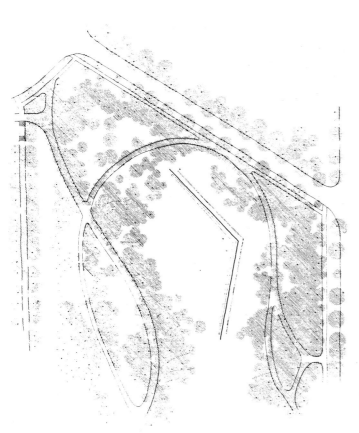

The design of the *VIETNAM VETERANS MEMORIAL* was the outcome of a design competition. *Maya Lin,* the sculptor who won this competition, chose not symbols, but a simple, stark, two-winged wall set into a v-shaped cleft as her design for the memorial. This man-made cleft was constructed in such a way that the visitor approaches the intersection of the two wings at the 10-foot-high juncture, then is free to tranverse either 200-foot-long segment.

Each of these segments — wings — points either to the Washington or the Lincoln Monument, symbolically tying those who died in the Vietnam War to the Fathers of Their Country. This general and somewhat esoteric symbolism is counterpointed by the engraving on the walls themselves. The black stone walls are divided into segments which are engraved with the names of 57,692 men and women who gave their lives in this war. This personalization is what makes this monument so powerful.

In most countries, including the United States, there are "Tombs to the Unknown Soldier." In many ways, the veterans of the Vietnam War were not only "unknown" soldiers, but also "unrecognized" soldiers.

This way of recognizing each individual by inscribing his or her name was a way of paying tribute to personal rather than national sacrifice — a concept important to this memorial. The scale of the stone wings also enforces this concept.

The change in scale created by sloping the earth down to the intersection of the wings takes you symbolically from the insignificant to the grand. All the while you're making the transition, however, the names engraved remind you that the transition was accomplished only by individuals.

This eloquent statement in stone, set in the grassy slopes of the nation's capital, stating not profound quotations, but only the names of the dead, recognizes the human need for remembrance, but also the need for reconciliation. The meeting of the earth, the engraved rock and the sky is a way to symbolize the possibility.

Project
Vietnam Veterans Memorial
Location
Washington, D.C., USA
Artist
Maya Lin

Remembering the Dead

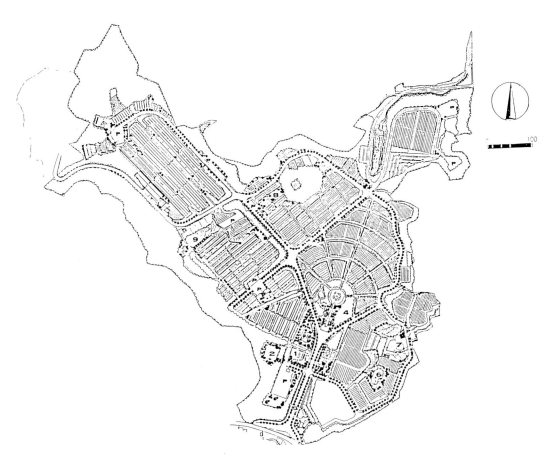

Burying the dead, honoring the dead, remembering the dead — all these acts are, for the most part, culturally determined. National heritage, religious beliefs, family traditions — all of these attributes could help to influence if, how and where you bury your dead. And the percentage of the population that shares these attributes could help to determine the type of cemetery in or around your community.

In Japan, in Shimotawara, Shijonawate-shi, Oska Prefecture, landscape architects *Haruto Kobayashi + TLA* have designed *IIMORI CEMETERY PARK* at the foot of the Ikoma Mountain Range. This cemetery was designed to have "an image of a serene garden." How do you design an image? What is the image of a "serene garden?" Tranquility and dignity are two aspects of serene. If one studies the plan of Iimori Cemetery, one is aware of the sense of dignity in the formal, processional approach to the cemetery.

The flowering cherry trees along this processional avenue are distinctively Japanese. One thinks of a Japanese cemetery. Along with this, however, is another aspect of this space: recreational space seems inherent in this design in the artificial water areas and small gardens that are interspersed throughout the design. This sense of recreation is deliberate. The designers specifically designed spaces for the recreational needs of the community. This area serves not only as the community's cemetery, it also serves as a recreational space.

There are also corners for remembrance built into this design. The wooded area named "Yasuragi-no-mori" has many such corners. The streams and fountains in

Siting this place for burial at the foot of the mountain range, providing streams, fountains and gardens for rest and contemplation does give comfort to the grieving. In addition, it provides a place for communion with nature and for recreational needs. In a true community sense, the designers have provided a space for solace, peace and continuity. The cherry trees viewed as they are in their seasonal garb must remind those who approach of the cycles and seasons of nature and life.

this area are designed to convey the image of the "home of the spirit." Surely many friends and relatives who have loved ones buried here might feel that was a fitting image for this space. The abundance of natural beauty also might contribute to this image.

Project
Imori Cemetery Park
Location
Shimotaware, Shijonawate-shi, Osaka Pref., Japan
Client
Imori Cemetery Park Association
Landscape Architect
Tokyo Landscape Architects Inc., Haruto Kobayashi
Photographer
© Tokyo Landscape Architects Inc., Haruto Kobayashi

A Renaissance Concept

The firm of *Edward Larrabee Barnes/ John M.Y. Lee, Architects* (*Alistair Bevington,* principal-in-charge of the design team) designed the *MINNEAPOLIS SCULPTURE GARDEN/SAGE AND JOHN COWLES CONSERVATORY. Quennell Rothschild Associates* were the landscape architects for the Sculpture Garden, and *Michael Valkenburgh/Barbara Solomon* designed the landscape architecture for the interior of Cowles Conservatory. Siah Armajani was responsible for the design of the pedestrian bridge. The artists whose sculpture is featured are many, with

perhaps one of the most predominant pieces being the whimsical one by Claes Oldenburg at the north end of the axis.

The plan of the space would be described as a Renaissance axial plan, with one axis tying the gardens to the museum and the other tying the gardens to the conservatory. The clipped clear cedar hedges frame four outdoor "rooms" — "galleries." The paths allow the visitor not just to enter the outdoor "gallery," but also to stroll around the perimeter of the square

space and view the sculpture from all sides. This sense of both intimate viewing and grand vista is what creates the pattern and interaction of this formal viewing space.

When traversing the total space — the sculpture garden — the visitor has a sense of encounter. Nothing is fully seen or exposed until one is beyond the hedge barrier or the glass wall. Elements seen through or over a "wall" hint at what is to

come. But nothing is fully exposed. The viewer is tantalized, drawn forward to see the whole.

And yet the arrangement, the formality, seems to speak of simplicity and repose. The simplicity of the planting materials is partly responsible for this. The hedges, grassed areas and paths are only backdrop. The sculptures themselves are the central focus. They are, for the most part, contemporary sculptures whose meaning and being are not immediately accessible. All the more reason to provide only non-obtrusive background and directional elements. All the more reason

to provide a garden that does not compete with the sculptures — a design that has its roots not in the present, but in the ordered past.

Inside the glass "rooms," the same seems to be true. The ordered past — a space reminiscent of the Crystal Palace —

provides a setting for a tall palm garden surrounding a fish tank by Frank Gehry. The plantings in the wings of this light structure highlight and lead into this space. Outside, the space also leads to other sights and other panoramas.

A walkway and Siah Armajani's pedestrian bridge lead out of the sculpture garden, over the interstate expressway to Loring Park. This beautiful space (designed by Frederick Law Olmsted), is an element in the link between the Walker Art Center and the City of Minneapolis.

Project
Minneapolis Sculpture Garden
Location
Minneapolis, Minnesota, USA
Client
Minneapolis Park and Recreation Board
Design Firm
Edward Larrabee Barnes/John M.Y. Lee, Architects: Alistair Bevington, principal-in-charge
Landscape Architect
Quennell Rothschild Associates
Photographers
Richard Payne, Mark Darley
Consultants
Michael Van Valkenburgh/Barbara Solomon, Cowles Conservatory interiors; Weidlinger Associates, and Bakke, Kopp, Ballou & McFarlin, structural engineers

The Relationship Between Sculpture & Space

Isamu Noguchi was originally commissioned to do only the Patio des Delegues, a triangular shaped outdoor "room" at UNESCO Headquarters in Paris. Because this area seemed to have no relationship to another garden space — a sunken area on the other side of the building intended for a Calder sculpture — Noguchi proposed creating a design that would correlate and connect the two spaces. The resulting design, the GARDENS FOR UNESCO, not only connects and correlates the spaces, but adds still a further dimension to the UNESCO grounds — what might be called an ambulatory garden.

In this garden one must walk through the space, on and over the stones, in order to understand and perceive the spatial nuances, the light, the values, textures and rhythms of these carefully chosen and placed rocks, plant materials and water areas. In effect, each element (perhaps especially each rock) becomes a sculptural form. In order to achieve this exquisite placement and counterpoint of texture, movement and color, Isamu Noguchi went to Japan to personally choose and cut the stones for this installation. Since he conceived of risks as essential to the fulfillment of his design

concept and UNESCO had no budget for rocks of this type and size, he suggested that the Japanese donate the rocks.

In fact, the Japanese were delighted to do so, and donated rocks from a mountain area on the island of Shikoku ("the blue stone of Io" from along the river Ayuu-Kui-Gawa), water basins and stepping-stones from Kyoto, quarried and carved stone for stepping-stones, stone lanterns and the stone bridge from Shodo Island. These were transported back to Paris where, with some difficulty (two Japanese gardeners were sent for), the stones were installed along with plant materials from Japan — cherry trees, dwarf bamboo, camellia and decorative maples.

The lower area of the gardens is called Jardin Japonais. This area seems more directly derivative of the traditional Japanese garden than the other parts of the installation. Noguchi acknowledges that the inspiration for this space most

certainly was the Japanese tradition. However, the composition and sculptural placement of the rocks is very much his own. The rocks are the lines, the skeleton, the structure of his design. In Japan rocks are called the "bones" of the garden. When all planting has died, the rocks will still show the quality and form of the garden.

The true Japanese tradition also allows for the greatest latitude. Noguchi did not want to do a totally Japanese composition, feeling that it was not in scale with the surrounding buildings. That would seem to be one of the problems of garden design in the twentieth century.

Since gardens by their nature express the continuity of time and the leisure to

pursue the inner needs of man — contemplation, inner purpose, timelessness — they are in direct contrast to most twentieth-century buildings which express purpose, industry, economic growth, trade and expansion. Perhaps that is why gardens like the Gardens for UNESCO are so important. In the midst of industry and purpose, modern man needs time and place to contemplate his goals.

Project
Gardens for UNESCO
Location
Paris, France
Client
UNESCO
Sculptor
Isamu Noguchi
Photographer
Isamu Noguchi

A Minimalist Approach

When it was suggested to *Isamu Noguchi* by Henry Segerstrom (Prudential Insurance) that he design a fountain for a small park, he requested certain conditions — a great, bare, cubic space for an ideal composition was to be made available. This was agreed to and the resulting design is a symbol both of the climate and topography of the area — Costa Mesa, California, and of the "true confluence of interest" of the sculptor and the client.

The minimalist feeling of this elegantly articulated, small, walled space could be said to have been inspired by the semi-arid, coastal location of this sculpture and multi-use garden. Here the sea meets the sand, the sand meets the arid soil with

small plants struggling for survival, the arid soil meets the developments. Nothing of this area is lush, save the sea. When one contemplates what Noguchi has achieved in this design one thinks of aridity, sparseness, drought, sun, ebbing, flowing — the attributes of this Southern California coastal town.

The installation is composed within a walled compound paved with irregular stones the color of sand. A small dome, a mini-hill, erupts from the paving. Minimal planting graces this form and the perimeter of the space. A winding, appearing,

disappearing, snake-like "stream-bed"
crosses the court in a meandering fashion.
Yet each component of this element is
perfectly placed. Large natural rocks are
interspersed with hard-edged polished
stone forms and surfaces — again
perfectly composed.

One has the feeling both of control and
serenity in this garden. Nothing is out of
place, so the design is complete. Yet one
wonders how the randomness of human
habitation will alter the space. Cut off from
adjacent, extraneous influences, the space
is a refuge, an oasis. Yet the very

perfectness of it might be intimidating. On
the other hand, the perfect placement of
each element is a positive counterpoint to
the chaos of freeways, air pollution and
stress.

Project
California Scenario
Location
Costa Mesa, California, USA
Client
Henry Segerstrom/Prudential Insurance
Design Firm
Isamu Noguchi, sculptor; Fuller & Sado,
architects
Photographer
Gary McKinnis
Consultants
Kammire, landscape; Fisher Marantz, lighting;
Dick Chaix, fountain

Symbiosis of Past, Present & Future

This Japanese garden and tearoom was designed to be installed on the 11th floor of a condominium in the heart of Tokyo. This rooftop garden space — *YUISHIKIAN* — with its reproduction of a sixteenth-century teahouse, Kan'un-ken (by Kobori Enshu), and the beautifully articulated traditional arrangement of stones and plantings is an oasis for architect *Kisho*

Kurokawa. Here, in the midst of urban chaos and pollution, he has designed and installed an environment that brings his heritage to life.

This traditional heritage, with the dark stones set to emulate a gently flowing stream, provides a mini-environment of calm, quiet and order. One seems to have

stepped into Tokyo of the past by simply passing through the door of the teahouse. Yet from the window of the teahouse, one can see the high-rise buildings of the

Tokyo of today. Visually, they co-exist side by side.

Kurokawa's residence adjoins this gentle garden space. His computer room is also adjacent. His comment on this tangential quality of the past and present is that this arrangement reflects his philosophy — "the Symbiosis of Tradition and High-technology." This inclusion of past and present, this linking of the old with the new culture, is perhaps indicative of the more sensitive and viable design of the future. Each design form has its reason and its season; one must always learn from the past to go forward into the future.

Project
Yuishikian
Location
Tokyo, Japan
Design Firm
Kisho Kurokawa Architect & Associates

A Satire For Genetics

Martha Schwartz was commissioned by Nobel Prize-winner David Baltimore (director of the Institute) to do a rooftop garden for the Whitehead Institute for Biomedical Research in Cambridge, Massachusetts. The resulting installation — the *"SPLICE GARDEN"* — was to be part of their art collection and was to serve two purposes: an outdoor extension of the adjacent faculty lounge, and a visual extension of a student classroom.

There are many who feel that the role of the artist is to comment on and critique society, to point out fallacies, follies and injustices. Martha Schwartz adopted this role when she designed this rooftop space. Playing on the term "gene-splicing"

and on the location of the institute — A-I (artificial intelligence) Alley — she opted to design a garden "spliced" together from two different cultures and created from artificial materials.

The "splicing" of the garden across the diagonal of the 25' x 30' space is done with a "line" of black-painted steel filled with black sand. This visual division separates the "French" garden of lush, dense, somewhat functional elements from the Japanese "Zen" garden, with its minimal elements selectively placed in the carefully raked green gravel. It is the "French" garden that is used by the faculty

for sitting, eating lunch and sunning themselves. The "Zen" garden with its unlikely topiary plants (the "French" influence transplanted) is left undisturbed, used for contemplation perhaps in the same way as is its inspirational source.

The inspirational source of the total garden — artificial means of creating life — is carried out not just in the symbolism but in the materials. There is no life on this barren rooftop. All the materials are artificial. The stylized hedges of the "French" garden are rolled steel covered with Astroturf, the topiary plants are plastic. Yet, the varying shades of green in this exquisitely designed space challenge the viewer to believe that these are live plants, that this, indeed, is a real roof garden. The puzzle is set forth to solve — what does constitute life?

The ability to sustain life is part of the puzzle of life and living matter. On this rooftop there are conditions that preclude

the use of living plants — the structure of the building cannot support the additional weight of soil or water. Therefore, there are no living plants, only lightweight, indestructible, make-believe plants. The continuation of the species is impossible on this rooftop. Perhaps that is the conundrum of the Institute.

Project
Whitehead Institute "Splice Garden"
Location
Cambridge, Massachusetts, USA
Design Firm
Martha Schwartz, Artist
Photographer
Alan Ward
Consultants
William Fuss & Son, artifical plant fabricator;
Terry Lee Dill, Robert Scheffman, contractors

Predictions for the Future

The highest good is like water. Water benefits all things generously and is without strife. It dwells in the lowly places that men disdain. Thus it comes near to the Tao. The highest good love the [lowly] earth for its dwelling. It loves the profound in its heart, it loves humanity in friendship, sincerity in speech, order in government, effectiveness in deeds, timeliness in action. Since it is without strife, it is without reproach.

Lao Tzu in the Tao Te Ching

By 'sense of the earth' we mean here the passionate sense of common destiny that draws the thinking fraction of life ever further forward. Rightly, no feeling is better founded in nature and therefore more powerful, than this one. But in fact, none is slower to awake either, since in order to become explicit, it requires that our consciousness, rising above the growing (but still much too limited) circles of family, country and race, shall finally discover that the only truly natural and real human unity is the spirit of the earth.

Human Energy
Pierre Teilhard de Chardin; A Helen and Kurt Wolff Book, Harcourt Brace Jovanovich, Inc., New York 1969

... I have learned that one of the creatures most acutely aware of the passing of time is the fiddler crab himself. Tiny spots on his body enlarge during daytime hours, giving him the same color as the mudbank he explores and thus protecting him from his enemies. At night the spots shrink, his color fades, and he is almost invisible in the light of the moon. These changes are synchronized with the tides, so that each day they occur at a different hour. A scientist who experimented with the crabs to learn more about the phenomenon discovered that even when they are removed from their natural environment and held in confinement, the rhythm of their bodily changes continues uninterrupted, and they mark the passage of time in their laboratory prison, faithful to the tides in their fashion.

"The Ring of Time" from Essays of E.B. White
Harper & Row Publishers, New York 1977

Time and movement in landscape design are inexorable. Nothing man can do (short of creating a landscape design of man-made materials, and even many of these materials are subject to decay and decomposition) can alter the fact that plant materials have their cycles and growing seasons, rocks and earth erode and change and water is never still, never static. Even a still pond water is in flux in its silent evaporation. Time and movement are essential components of the landscape design process. One might say that the designers who are the most successful are those who use those attributes to the fullest extent possible.

The revolutions of the earth, the juxtaposition of the planets, climatic changes, growing cycles, movement of wind and water — all these elements give landscape design a vitality and strength that combines with a vulnerability to the natural elements to give each project a sense of impermanence and tension. This razor's edge, so to speak, of a superb installation that could be destroyed in the next hurricane, tornado, hail storm or drought is the essence of the difference between the growing environment and the substantially man-made environment.

In many of our examples, however, the natural, the cultivated environment is interrelated with the man-made environment in a happy symbiosis. These examples are perhaps less vulnerable to the elements. Here again, however, it takes the sensitive designer who understands both plant materials and structure to create these environments where neither man-made nor the natural takes precedent and appears to overshadow the other. The two aspects of the design are in balance. When you experience the design, there's nothing you would add and nothing you would take away. This concept, of course, is one definition of an aesthetic experience. One might say that balance is the key.

Altering Nature — The Ultimate Balancing Act

In the examples we've used to illustrate the different aspects of landscape design, we've employed a number of elements to help the reader understand and relate to the projects. The materials the designer has to work with — plant materials, earth, rock, water, man-made materials — are the essential and perhaps the most tangible elements. Each of these components one can pick up and hold in one's hand. It's also possible to go out into any natural landscape and probably find all of them — even the man-made materials. Bottles, cans and other bits of man's discards are more and more making their way into the remote areas of the earth.

The design components we've employed — Space, Mass, Line & Direction, Color, Light Shade, Texture, Scent, Time, Movement — are more abstract and more arbitrary. When one speaks of balance in a design, these abstract concepts become very useful tools, but only if one understands that they are abstract and often employed subjectively — except for the concepts of Time and Movement.

Even if the example of landscape design one is trying to explain is a paved plaza with no water, no plant materials, Time and Movement are essential factors. People entering and leaving the plaza would create movement. The earth would be moving around the sun and the light and shadows would change. Wind would create movement. Perhaps a sealed room in the interior of a building would not be subjected to Time and Movement, but anything outside, any installation beyond the exterior walls of the building is subject to these essential components.

How to make the most of these components is, of course, how you create that synthesis of aesthetics and technology by using Rhythm & Balance, Unity & Variety, Accent & Contrast, Scale & Proportion. If you notice, all of these elements are antithetical — the Yin and the Yang. Once again we are back to "balance" being a key in landscape design. Perhaps the person who understands the essence of balance possesses that indefinable element of talent to create those landscape designs that are timeless and memorable.

Since most of the designs we've used have been created within the last 20-25 years it's difficult to say which among them will be lasting. Some, however, seem to have that essence, that sense that at least a hundred years from now they will still exist, still be viable. But a landscape design is, by its nature, not as permanent, not as lasting as an architectural design. At least not without continued maintenance and care.

Defining Stewardship

Maintenance and care — stewardship, management, if you will — is a necessary consideration in landscape design. Granted, wilderness seems to care for itself without the intervention of man. When there are forest fires, droughts, volcanic explosions, hurricanes, tornados, nature eventually renews itself. But here we are speaking of unaltered nature — nature without the artificial intervention of man. It would be possible to postulate here that even the gardens created by man would renew themselves and grow again after a disaster. And probably in some ways they would. The difference, however, is that the way in which they would renew themselves would perhaps not be in quite the way the designer envisioned the renewal. Unless, of course, this aspect was built into the design.

How does one build renewal, restoration into design? Is it possible to alter the environment and yet create a self-sustaining, self-renewing installation? It's an interesting question to contemplate. I think the answer would be yes, only if you could incorporate the element of evolutionary time and understand that each renewal would alter the original. Once again we return to the concept of time and the landscape.

At this point, let's touch on another aspect of time. Let's explore time as a limited entity, interrelated with resources as a limited entity, and return to stewardship of the planet. The Judeo-Christian view of both time and resources seems to have been that the world was given to man with all its bounty to use forever, or at least until Judgment Day or whatever event would be the end of the earth. Stewardship, in this sense, was use of and not conservation of — spending, not saving or conserving.

The eastern concept (perhaps most specifically the Taoist) seems to be that man and the elements of nature are all equal inhabitants of the planet. This being a rather crowded planet, it makes more sense to provide room for everyone. It also pays to respect each other. Balance, the Yin and Yang, come into play in this concept. Man is not the master, he is a responsible participant. Which concept is the better one? Each person may have a different answer to that question, but some things seem rather clear. Nature is a powerful force and how we deal with nature seems to depend on the social mores of the time.

Sociological Shift from Domination to Conservation

In this book, So *Human An Animal* (Charles Scribner's Sons, 1968), Rene Dubos makes these two statements:

One of the reasons for the emotional impoverishment in countries where industry and technology have taken over is the loss of identification with the natural world. Increasingly we tend to deal with nature as if it were of value only as a source of raw material and entertainment.

Whether man considers himself part of nature, or outside of it and its master, is determined not by racial origins, but by cultural forces.

Another aspect of time to be considered is the time we live in and the social mores and cultural forces of that time. If we consider the last 20-25 years, as illustrated by the examples in this book, it would seem to be a fairly auspicious time for landscape design. Certainly a great many large projects have been funded. In that sense, it has the feel of a kind of renaissance. Also, there are some humanistic aspects — the quality of life and the necessity of integrating the natural environment into the technological and corporate environment for physical and mental health — in many of the large-scale designs funded by industry and corporations. Not to mention the renaissance of the environmental movement. Conserving and preserving the environment for future generations seems to be a prevalent theme in many of the designs. Also, revitalization of under-used and abandoned areas is a kind of renaissance.

The times we live in seem to be auspicious in these particular aspects. We seem, even on a global scale, to be learning some lessons about the landscape. At least there are those at a national level who are speaking to

each other about the problems and suggesting solutions. Those engaging in these dialogues are also from different cultures and geologically different parts of the globe. This in itself is very hopeful. It proposes the possibility of a certain universality to this renaissance of the natural as opposed to the technological — this renaissance of man as a part of, not master of nature.

A Universality of Language

In as much as possible, the examples in this book are from diverse areas of the globe. There are obviously cultural differences evident in certain forms of the design. There are those examples where one can point and say, "Oh, this is an English garden," or, "This is a Japanese garden." But not in as many instances as one might imagine. It's an interesting phenomenon that the visual language of landscape design is extremely universal. Consider the symbols all landscape designers use — plant materials, earth forms, water, rocks — the majority of these symbolic elements exist everywhere on the globe. Certainly when one looks at the plan for landscape design, the language of the words is irrelevant. The symbols give you the outline of the story. And the final installation gives the whole volume, word by word. Without the benefit of translation. In that, the landscape design is timeless.

Nature is also timeless. Long after man has left the earth — if destruction of the planet, indeed, becomes man's choice — nature will probably survive, but in new and evolutionary forms. When the dinosaurs roamed the planet, plant materials were not what they are today. But they evolved, they adapted. Perhaps better than man. It might be well to remember that lesson.

Plants are fragile: they can die from lack of care, lack of sunlight and lack of water. But they also can spring to life again with just a little water — the rainstorm in the desert that brings it to life. Man, on the other hand, is not quite so capable of lying dormant until auspicious circumstances make it possible to grow and bloom again. It just might be that nature has the edge over us. We might also consider that nature not only has the edge over us, it's necessary for our survival. Without plant life, how will we manufacture enough oxygen to maintain our planet?

INDEX

PROJECTS

FIRMS

ARTISTS/SCULPTORS

CLIENTS